RISING STARS

The 10 Best Young Players in Baseball

Alan Schwarz

Sports Illustrated
KiDS
B O O K S

This Library Edition First Published and Exclusively Distributed by
The Rosen Publishing Group, Inc.
New York

Alan Schwarz is a national columnist for Baseball America.
He frequently writes about baseball for SPORTS ILLUSTRATED FOR KIDS *magazine.*

This library edition first published in 2003 and exclusively distributed
by The Rosen Publishing Group, Inc., New York

Copyright © 2003 SPORTS ILLUSTRATED FOR KIDS Books

Book Design: Michelle Innes
Additional editorial material: Jennifer Silate and Nel Yomtov
Originally edited by Ron Berler

Photo Credits: Cover (right), pp. 29, 45, 49, 87, 127 © David Seelig/Icon SMI;
cover (left and center), pp. 7, 13, 21, 57, 93, 101, 107 © Chuck Solomon/SI/Icon
SMI; introduction page, chapter start pages, career stat pages, and background
images © Photodisc; pp. 23, 63, 71, 133 © Reuters NewMedia Inc./CORBIS;
p. 37 © John Biever/SI/Icon SMI; p. 51 © ALLSPORT; p. 65 © Jeff Carlick/Icon
SMI; pp. 79, 91, 105, 119, 121 © John Cordes/Icon SMI; p. 113 © Dale
Zanine/Icon SMI; pp. 135, 143 © John Iacono/SI/Icon SMI; p. 149 © Joe
Robbins/Icon SMI

First Edition

Library of Congress Cataloging-in-Publication Data

Schwarz, Alan.
    Rising stars : the 10 best young players in baseball / by Alan Schwarz.
        p. cm.
    "Sports illustrated for kids books."
    Includes index.
        ISBN 0-8239-3576-0 (lib. bdg.)
        1. Baseball players–Rating of. I. Title.

GV865 .A1 S335 2003
796.357'092'273–dc21
                                                        2001005593

CONTENTS

>> INTRODUCTION

One of the best things about being a baseball fan is watching young players blossom into superstars. At the beginning of the 1990s, current superstars such as Ken Griffey, Jr., and Greg Maddux were young and just beginning to dominate the major leagues. Now, as the next decade gets under way, another generation of talented young players are making names for themselves. You'll meet 10 of those players in *Rising Stars*.

Our lineup includes three super shortstops — Derek Jeter of the New York Yankees, Nomar Garciaparra of the Boston Red Sox, and Alex Rodriguez of the Texas Rangers — and a trio of awesome outfielders: Andruw Jones of the Atlanta Braves, Vladimir Guerrero of the Montreal Expos, and Shawn Green of the Los Angeles Dodgers. At the plate stands one of baseball's best pure hitters: Sean Casey, the first baseman for the Cincinnati Reds. Behind the plate is turbocharged catcher Jason Kendall of the Pittsburgh Pirates. On the mound is pitcher Kevin Millwood of the Atlanta Braves, and out in the bullpen you'll find flamethrowing closer Billy Wagner of the Houston Astros.

Turn the page and read about the challenges these 10 players faced on the road to the big leagues, the dedication that it took for them to succeed, and why they will be making headlines for many seasons to come.

>>DEREK JETER

Every season's a dream for this dandy Yankee

In Derek Jeter's eighth-grade yearbook, kids at St. Augustine Cathedral School in Kalamazoo, Michigan, made predictions about what they would someday be. Some kids said they would be doctors. Others said they would be lawyers. Derek said he would be the shortstop for the New York Yankees.

"I was always telling people that I was going to play for the Yankees someday," says Derek, who constantly wore his navy blue Yankee cap, Yankee jacket, and prized gold Yankee medallion. He lay on his bed at night and imagined himself scooping up grounders in front of a cheering crowd at Yankee Stadium and firing throws to first base.

stat city

DEREK JETER

TEAM	New York Yankees
POSITION	Shortstop
ACQUIRED	Chosen by the Yankees in the first round (6th player chosen overall) of the major league draft on June 1, 1992
BORN	June 26, 1974, in Pequannock, New Jersey
HEIGHT	6′ 3″
WEIGHT	195 pounds
BATS	Right
THROWS	Right
BIG FEAT	In 1998, Derek joined Phil Rizzuto as the only Yankee shortstops who have rapped 200 or more hits in a season. Phil did it in 1950. Derek repeated the feat in 1999 and 2000.
HONORS	A.L. All-Star, 2001, 2000, 1999, 1998; World Series Most Valuable Player, 2000; All-Star Game Most Valuable Player, 2000; A.L. Rookie of the Year, 1996

Derek's prediction — and fondest dream — came true eight years later when the Yankees called him up from the minor leagues to be their shortstop. He has been having dream seasons ever since.

During his first full season, Derek won the 1996 American League (A.L.) Rookie of the Year award and was a spark plug in the Yankees' World Series championship. In 1998, he became an All-Star for the first time. He hit .324 and stole 30 bases while the Yanks won a major league record total of 125 games, and another World Series. He hit .349 during the 1999 regular season and .353 during New York's four-game Series sweep of the Atlanta Braves. Many people called him the best young player in baseball.

"Derek is the best player I've ever played with, and I think a lot of people in this clubhouse are going to say that before he's done," says former Yankee rightfielder Paul O'Neill. Paul joined the major leagues in 1985, so he has played with a lot of good players. "What sets Derek apart is the number of ways he can affect a game," says Paul.

Derek is a complete package of all-around skills. He can hit for average, drive in runs, knock an occasional home run, and steal bases. He takes particular pride in his slick fielding. He dives all over the infield for ground balls and makes spectacular throws.

"I think defense wins games," says Derek. "I don't care how many home runs you hit or how many runs batted in (RBIs) you have. If you're out there giving the runs away on defense, your homers and RBIs don't help a whole lot. I think defense should be the first thing you talk about."

Well, the first thing people usually talk about is Derek's knack for achieving great things.

GRANDMA'S GIFT

Derek was born on June 26, 1974, in Pequannock, New Jersey. His family later moved to Kalamazoo, Michigan. Derek often spent his summer vacations in West Milford, New Jersey, with his grandmother Dot.

Dot loved the Yankees. She told Derek about the many times she went to Yankee Stadium as a kid in the 1930s to watch the great centerfielder Joe DiMaggio. Her stories made Derek a Yankee fan, too. He and Grandma Dot went to games at Yankee Stadium together, and he dreamed about playing for the Yankees.

Derek had a lot of natural baseball talent, but he worked hard to make the most of it. "Baseball is not an easy sport," he says. "My parents taught me that the harder you work, the better you'll be."

By the time Derek was a senior at Kalamazoo Central High School, scouts from the Yankees and other major league teams had their eyes on him. Derek missed much of his senior season with an ankle injury but still wowed the scouts with his eye-popping .508 batting average.

When the 1992 major league draft was held in early June, Derek could have been picked by the Houston Astros, Cincinnati Reds, or three other teams. All five teams chose ahead of the Yankees. All five took other players. The Yankees gladly chose Derek. He made their pick look good by improving rapidly. He won the 1994 Minor League Player of the Year award by hitting a total average of .344 at three levels of the Yankees' organization: A, AA, and AAA!

The following season, Derek's dream came true — for a while, anyway. He was promoted to the Yankees on May 29 at the ripe old age of 20. The Yankees' starting shortstop had been injured, so Derek took his place. He played in 13 games and hit .234 before being sent back to the minors on June 11.

Derek made the Yankees for good during spring training of 1996. He wasn't expected to play the entire season with the team, but he quickly proved he was just too good to send back to the minors. On Opening Day, Derek smacked a home run at Jacobs Field in Cleveland, Ohio. He hit .314 and was named A.L. Rookie of the Year that season. Derek had become a star.

THE SPARK PLUG

Derek was the team's spark plug as the Yankees drove to their first World Series since 1978. Yankee fans will never forget one of his at-bats in Game 1 of the 1996 American League Championship Series (ALCS), against the Baltimore Orioles at Yankee Stadium in the Bronx, New York.

Derek tied the score at 4–4 by hitting a clutch home

run in the bottom of the eighth inning. Well, it was *sort* of a home run. Derek's blast was caught by a young fan who reached over the right field fence and snatched the ball before the Oriole rightfielder could catch it! The umpires ruled it a home run. The Yanks went on to win, 5–4, in 11 innings. They later took the ALCS, four games to one. Then they went on to beat the Atlanta Braves in six games in the World Series.

MR. POPULAR

Derek quickly became the most popular Yankee. He received piles of fan mail each week, not only because he's a great player but also because he's a likable person. He's polite, friendly, and a good teammate. He also has movie-star looks and a smile that makes girls swoon. At Yankee Stadium, girls wave signs that say "I Love You, Derek" and "Derek, Will You Marry Me?" He can't go anywhere in New York City without attracting a crowd.

"Going out on the town with Derek is like going out with Elvis Presley," says Yankee third baseman Scott Brosius.

Derek says he likes to keep his life quiet and stay home in his New York City apartment. "I'm a big movie fan. That's basically what I do every night, even in the off-season. Dinner and a movie — that's good enough for me."

Derek also likes to help people. In 1996, he started the Turn 2 Foundation, which raises money to fight drug

Derek Jeter

Derek's range and sure-handed fielding make him one of the best glovemen in major league baseball.

and alcohol use among young people. "I think it's a great cause," says Derek. "I want to show kids that there's another way to go."

The Turn 2 Foundation is named after the baseball term for turning a double play on defense — something good shortstops like Derek do often. The Foundation has raised almost $1 million to help kids in New York City and Kalamazoo, Michigan, stay away from drugs and alcohol. The money is also used to create college scholarships for deserving high school students in both of those cities.

Derek got the idea for starting his own foundation from baseball Hall of Famer Dave Winfield. Dave was an All-Star outfielder for the Yankees in the 1980s and Derek's favorite player. Dave had his own charity foundation, and Derek wanted to follow in Dave's footsteps.

"I thought it was cool that Dave took the time out of his schedule to help people," says Derek. "I told my dad that if I ever made it, I wanted to do the same thing."

NEVER CONTENT

Derek improved steadily each year following his excellent rookie season in 1996. He hit .291 in 1997 and made great strides with his fielding, but the Yankees were eliminated by the Cleveland Indians in the A.L. Division Series. In 1998, Derek really teed off at the plate.

He batted .324, with 19 homers and 84 RBIs. He also led the A.L. in runs scored, with 127.

Derek had a dazzling season in 1999. He played in his second All-Star Game, led the league with 219 hits, and was second in average (.349), runs (134), and triples (9). He also drove in a career-high 102 runs.

Derek continued to shine in the World Series. He batted .353, stole three bases, and scored four runs as the Yankees blew away the Braves in four games. Derek had won his third World Series ring in four seasons!

"If Derek didn't win the World Series each year, he'd probably go home and cry and wonder what went wrong," joked Chili Davis, who was the Yankee designated hitter that season.

"This is special," Derek told reporters. "Every championship is great. Every year is a different story."

The story got even better for Derek in the 2000 season. Although he played in only 148 games — his fewest since becoming the Yankees' regular shortstop — Derek had another solid year. He batted .339 with 15 home runs, 73 RBIs, and 201 hits.

Derek was continuing to add his name to the long list of all-time Yankee greats. He became only the third Yankee to have three 200-hit seasons in a row, joining Lou Gehrig (1927–1929) and Don Mattingly (1984–1986). Against the Detroit Tigers on September 25, Derek got his 1000th career hit. At 26, he became the second youngest Yankee ever to do this. Only Mickey Mantle, at age 25, was younger when he accomplished this feat.

Hall of Fame DOUBLE

Joe Cronin was not just a great player. Like Derek, he was also a great leader. Joe played shortstop, mostly for the Washington Senators and Boston Red Sox from 1926 to 1945. He was a wonderful hitter who batted .301 for his career, and drove in more than 100 runs in a season eight times. He was such a good leader that he was hired as the Senators' manager in 1933 — at the age of 27 — and led Washington to the American League pennant that year.

A SHINING STAR

Derek is used to playing in front of large crowds and television audiences. The pressure just doesn't seem to bother him. In fact, he seems to thrive in those kinds of situations. When shortstop Alex Rodriguez of the Seattle Mariners was injured and unable to play in the 2000 All-Star Game in Atlanta, Georgia, Derek was chosen to start in his place for the A.L. In front of a packed stadium and with millions watching the game around the world on TV, Derek went three for three and led the American League to a 4–1 victory.

Derek's performance wowed fans and fellow players. The Cubs' Joe Girardi, Derek's former Yankee teammate, said, "He's a special player . . . most people don't get to the level he plays at." Girardi wasn't the only one to think so. Derek was selected the Most Valuable Player (MVP) of the All–Star Game, becoming the first Yankee ever to receive the honor. His bat was sent to the Baseball Hall of Fame in Cooperstown, New York, after the game ended.

PENNANT FEVER

Derek and the Yankees had their eyes on another World Series ring in 2000. No team had won three straight championships since the Oakland Athletics in the early 1970s. Critics of the Yankees said that the team had gotten too old and that some of the players wouldn't perform well down the stretch run. The critics were almost proven right as the Yankees suffered through a terrible month of September, losing 15 of their last 18 games of the season.

However, the Yankees did make it to the playoffs and beat a solid, young Oakland Athletics team in the A.L. Division Series, three games to two. The Yanks then knocked off the Seattle Mariners in the ALCS, four games to two. The "old" Yankees were showing that they still had plenty of fight in them.

Derek batted .268 with seven runs, two home runs and seven RBIs in the two series. Not bad numbers, but the star shortstop was saving his best for the World Series — a match-up against the Yankees' crosstown rivals, the New York Mets. The highly publicized "Subway Series" was the first pairing of two New York teams since 1956 when the Yankees faced the Brooklyn Dodgers.

In Game 4 of the series, Derek drove Mets' pitcher Rick Reed's first pitch of the game into the seats to give the Yankees the win, putting them up in the Series, three games to one. In Game 5, the Mets had a 2-1 lead late in the game when Derek stepped to the plate. On a 2-0 count, he crushed an Al Leiter pitch into the Mets' bullpen. Derek had tied the game.

The Yanks later won the game and captured another title. Derek batted .409 with six runs and two home runs in the series. He was named the World Series MVP. Derek's heroics had lifted the Yankees to their fourth championship in five years.

Derek appreciated this World Series win more than any other. "I'd be lying if I said this one wasn't more gratifying. We struggled this year [and] had a tough time; we have had our bumps in the road. But we are here, sitting here [as champions] at the end of the year," he said.

A ROLLERCOASTER RIDE

Derek's off-season celebration took a backseat to a serious family matter. In November 2000, Derek learned that his 21-year-old sister, Sharlee, had cancer. Sharlee had to undergo six months of therapy. At first, Derek chose not to talk publicly about his sister's illness. He finally revealed the news in May 2001, when Sharlee was declared "cancer-free." He said that the reason why he decided to tell others at all was because it was "a success story."

The good news about Sharlee matched another feel-good story for Derek during the off-season. He became the second-highest paid player in baseball when he signed a 10-year, $189 million contract with the Yankees. Derek probably could have gotten more if he had signed with another team, but he wanted to remain in the Bronx. "I really felt there was no reason to see if the grass was greener on the other side [by looking to sign with another team] . . . my first choice would have been New York."

SPRING FEVER

Things started slowly for Derek in the 2001 season. In spring training, he injured his shoulder and had a bad throat infection. By the time he recovered, he had played in only six spring training games. Then, he hurt his right thigh, causing him to begin the 2001 regular season on the disabled list. He returned to action on April 17, missing almost three weeks of the season. However, by mid-June, he was back in form, hitting well and aggressively running the bases with 13 stolen bases in 14 attempts.

Derek was once again chosen by A.L. All-Star Game manager Joe Torre to be Alex Rodriguez's replacement when Alex couldn't make the game because of an injury. Derek made the most of the opportunity, hitting a home run off Chicago Cub pitcher Jon Lieber. The American League won the game, 6–3. It was Derek's first All-Star homer. It was also the first home run hit by a Yankee in an All-Star game since 1959, when Yogi Berra did it. Derek had made history again.

Derek and the Yankess made it to the World Series for the fourth straight season, but they lost to the Arizona Diamondbacks, four games to three. Derek wrapped up the 2001 season with a .311 batting average, 191 hits, and 110 runs scored.

In spite of his success and the attention he receives, Derek stays focused on baseball, even in the off-season. He bought a home in Tampa, Florida, where the Yankees hold their spring training camp, so that he can work out during the winter and stay on top of his game.

"You can never be content with how you're playing," says Derek. "If you are, you'll never improve. If you want to be one of the premier players, you have to want to improve your entire game — your offense, defense, baserunning. You have to continue to work hard."

After all, hard work is what dreams are made of.

Derek combines clutch hitting with slick fielding and a never-ending desire to improve his game.

>>KEVIN MILLWOOD

He's the newest ace on an awesome pitching staff

Kevin Millwood tried hard to keep his emotions under control as he took the mound against the Houston Astros. It was Game 2 of the 1999 National League (N.L) Division Series at Turner Field, in Atlanta. And it was the first playoff start of Kevin's major league career.

He was excited — and a little nervous.

The Braves really needed Kevin to pitch well. They had been soundly beaten, 6–1, in Game 1. If they didn't win this game, they would fall dangerously behind Houston, no wins to two losses, in the best-of–five-game series.

▶ KEVIN MILLWOOD

TEAM	Atlanta Braves
POSITION	Pitcher
ACQUIRED	Chosen by the Braves in the 11th round of the major league draft on June 3, 1993
BORN	December 24, 1974, in Gastonia, North Carolina
HEIGHT	6' 4"
WEIGHT	220 pounds
BATS	Right
THROWS	Right
BIG FEAT	Kevin gave up only one hit while beating the Pittsburgh Pirates, 6–0, on April 14, 1998. In that game, he became the first Brave pitcher ever to record as many as 13 strikeouts without walking a batter.
HONORS	N.L. All-Star, 1999

Kevin struggled at first. He fell behind in the count to the first three batters he faced. But he got out of the inning without giving up a walk or a hit. When he took the mound in the top of the second inning, the Braves had a 1–0 lead. It didn't last long. Astro third baseman Ken Caminiti drove one of Kevin's pitches over the wall for a game-tying home run.

KEEPING HIS COOL

Many young pitchers might have panicked after that. Not Kevin. He told himself to relax. Throwing with a nice, easy motion, he began to mix fastballs, sliders, and curves that kept the hard–hitting Astro batters off–balance. His control was nearly perfect as he retired the next 15 batters he faced. Meanwhile, the Braves broke the 1–1 tie with a run in the bottom of the sixth inning. Then they busted the game open with three more runs in the seventh. The best the Astros could do was put a runner on first base in the eighth inning when Brave third baseman Chipper Jones made an error.

When Astro outfielder Stan Javier made the final out in the top of the ninth inning, Kevin was rushed by his happy teammates. He had given up only one hit in the entire game to stop the Astros cold. The final score: 5–1. Kevin was the first pitcher in 32 years to give up only one hit while pitching a complete post–season game! Jim Lonborg of the Boston Red Sox had been the last to do it, in 1967.

"It was probably the biggest game I have pitched in," Kevin told reporters after the game. "I would have to say it is my best performance ever."

Inspired by Kevin, the Braves went on to beat the Astros in the next two games to take the series. Kevin later helped the Braves beat the New York Mets in the

National League Championship Series (NLCS) and reach the World Series.

It took Kevin only two seasons to become one of the best pitchers in the major leagues. During the 1999 regular season, he had a brilliant 18–7 record. His 2.68 earned run average (ERA) was second–best in the N.L. Only Randy Johnson of the Arizona Diamondbacks had a lower ERA (2.48). Kevin held opposing batters to a puny .202 batting average against him, the lowest in the league for any starting pitcher!

"I think Kevin is the Braves' best pitcher right now," said retired slugger Mark McGwire of the St. Louis Cardinals.

That's saying a lot. The Braves have one of the best pitching staffs of all time. It includes Greg Maddux, Tom Glavine, and John Smoltz, who have all won the Cy Young Award as the best pitcher in the N.L. Greg has won four Cy Young Awards, Tom has won two, and John one.

LATE BLOOMER

Kevin Millwood was born on December 24, 1974, in Gastonia, North Carolina. He grew up in nearby Bessemer City and played on the basketball and base- ball teams at Bessemer City High. He was a decent pitcher who threw a respectable 89–mile–per–hour fastball, but only a few pro scouts believed he would ever be good enough to pitch in the majors.

Kevin himself did not expect to be drafted after his senior season. When the major league draft was held in June 1993, he didn't sit by the phone and wait for a team to call and say that they had picked him. Instead, he went to the beach for a week with his friends.

Surprise! The Braves drafted Kevin, although they didn't select him until the 11th round. Still, Kevin signed a contract and became a professional baseball player!

The Braves didn't consider Kevin to be a top prospect, so they bounced him back and forth between starting and relieving during his first three minor league seasons. They wanted to see what he did best. It wasn't until he was given the chance to pitch regularly as a starter for the Class A Durham (North Carolina) Bulls, in 1996, that Kevin began to gain the confidence he needed to let his talent blossom.

Kevin began the next season (1997) at Double–A Greenville, in South Carolina. His record was only 3–5, but his 4.11 ERA was good enough to earn him a mid–season promotion to Triple–A Richmond, in Virginia.

LEARNING TO BELIEVE

It was at Richmond that Kevin had the good fortune of working with pitching coach Bill Fischer. Bill had helped Roger Clemens rise to superstardom with the Boston Red Sox in the 1980s.

"Fisch made me a little tougher," Kevin says. "I believed even more that I could pitch anywhere. That's a big part of being a big-leaguer, knowing that your stuff is good enough."

Indeed it was. Kevin went 7–0 in nine starts for Richmond. He was called up to the major leagues on July 12, 1997. Two days later, he made his big-league debut. It was in relief, but Kevin was credited with a win against the Philadelphia Phillies. Then he lost two of his first three starts and was sent back to the minors for two weeks in August.

Kevin refused to feel down about his demotion. When he returned to Atlanta, he finished the season with a 5–3 record and a 4.03 ERA for the Braves. More importantly, he had shown that he wasn't intimidated by pitching on a staff that had three famous aces on it.

"That has hurt some of the other young guys who have been through here," says Tom Glavine. "It's something they feel they have to live up to."

LEARNING FROM THE BEST

Kevin tried to learn all he could from his famous teammates. He asked them questions and soaked up information like a sponge. From Tom, Kevin learned a lot about how to keep hitters off-balance by changing speeds and throwing unexpected pitches. Greg Maddux gave Kevin tips on improving his control. John Smoltz is

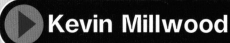
Kevin Millwood

Kevin became a polished pitcher by learning from his famous teammates, Greg Maddux, John Smoltz, and Tom Glavine.

a power pitcher like Kevin, so they talked about the best ways to overpower hitters.

Kevin became a polished mix of all three aces — a pitcher with smarts, control, and power. He joined the Braves' starting rotation at the beginning of the 1998 season and really did the job. He posted a sparkling 17–8 record with a 4.08 ERA. That was certainly a better start than some of his famous teammates had had. During *their* first full seasons in the majors, Greg Maddux had gone 6–14 (with the 1987 Chicago Cubs) and Tom Glavine had been 7–17 (with the 1988 Braves).

The highlight of Kevin's 1998 season came on April 14, when he pitched a one-hit shutout against the Pittsburgh Pirates at Turner Field. He struck out 13 batters and did not walk any. But Greg Maddux took Kevin aside after the game and told him: "That wasn't the most important game you've ever pitched. Your next one is."

Kevin used that lesson to make his 1999 season even more successful than 1998. He became almost unhittable at times, winning eight of his nine starts between May 17 and the All-Star Game on July 12. He was invited to Boston's Fenway Park to pitch for the National League in the All-Star Game. Kevin was the only Brave pitcher to make the N.L. squad!

"If someone had told me before the season started that I'd be the only pitcher on our staff to be here," Kevin told reporters, "I probably wouldn't have believed him."

SOMEDAY IS HERE

Kevin kept rolling after the All–Star break. In one stretch of four starts, he gave up just three hits in two of the games and two hits in the other two.

"I don't know how many games Kevin went into this year with no–hitters in the fourth inning, the fifth inning, the sixth inning," says Brave manager Bobby Cox. "Kevin really is a dominating pitcher."

As if his excellent regular season weren't enough, Kevin's masterful one–hitter against the Astros in the playoffs proved that he belonged on the great Brave staff, even if he is a bit too humble to come right out and say so.

UPS AND DOWNS

Following two strong seasons, Kevin struggled in 2000. He started strongly, winning his first three decisions. But after May 1, things took a downward turn as Kevin went 7–13 with a 5.14 ERA the rest of the season. Inconsistency plagued him as he finished at 10–13 with a 4.66 ERA. Kevin was allowing base runners to get on more than ever before — he surrendered more hits and more walks than in any of his previous seasons with the Braves.

After being beaten by the Florida Marlins in mid–May, Kevin, who knocked in a pair of runs in a losing cause, searched for an answer to his funk. "I would have traded a

Hall of Fame DOUBLE

Tom Seaver was a power pitcher with excellent control, and an ace his team could count on. "Tom Terrific" won 20 or more games in a season five times while pitching for the New York Mets, Cincinnati Reds, Chicago White Sox, and Boston Red Sox, from 1967 to 1986. He also led the National League in strikeouts five times, and once struck out 19 men in a game! Tom was elected to the Hall of Fame in 1992.

good night on the mound for a bad night at the plate. I'm struggling with my mechanics and fighting myself a bit," he said.

Kevin, who had never had a below-.500 winning percentage since he joined the Braves, didn't let his change of fortunes get him down. He knew what he had to do, it was just a matter of doing it. "I still have confidence in myself," Kevin said. "I know I can go out and win, but it just hasn't happened for me."

An easy answer never came for the struggling right-hander, but he did display flashes of his 1998 and 1999 brilliance in several outings. In a game against the Arizona Diamondbacks in early August, Kevin pitched the Braves to a 4–2 win, throwing 90 percent fastballs as he retired the first 13 batters he faced. "Millwood was the story tonight," said manager Cox. "I thought he was just great."

Later in the month, Kevin faced the Colorado Rockies at Coors Field, pitching seven strong innings. With his performance, Kevin had allowed only three earned runs in the last 20 innings he pitched. The victory evened his record at 8–8. Kevin was relieved that his luck might be changing. "It was nice to finally pick up a win and get back to .500 for the first time in a while."

Good luck didn't stay with Kevin for long as he went 2–5 the rest of the season. The slump that Kevin tried so hard to shake still had him in its grip. When the season ended, Kevin was glad his disappointing year was finally over. "The regular season is over for me, thank God. It pretty much stunk for me. I don't think I have helped this team as much as I was looked toward to do," he said.

But Kevin did have one more game to pitch in the 2000 season — against the powerhouse St. Louis Cardinals in the N.L. Division Series. Kevin got hit hard in the series' last game, giving up four runs on four hits and three walks. The Braves lost the game 3–1, and the Cardinals swept the best-of-five series, 3–0.

Kevin's long, frustrating season was finally over.

SPRING TRAINING BLUES

With the 2000 season behind him, Kevin headed into spring training for the 2001 season working to regain his form and his winning ways. It didn't happen. Kevin was hit hard in most of his outings and his frustration began to mount. In March, after a particularly rough day on the mound, he said, "I'm sick of this place [Florida spring training camp]. I really want to go home." Obviously, Kevin was ready for the season to begin. "Not until my turn comes up in April does it start counting," he added.

The regular season started and Kevin continued to struggle. On May 6, he left a game against the Cardinals after two innings because his right shoulder felt stiff. Of the discomfort, he said, "It's just kind of an ongoing thing. I've been fighting it since spring training. I thought I had it licked, but it never really went away." The next day, he was put on the disabled list for the first time in his career. Doctors later found a cyst in his shoulder. It kept him out of action for 75 days.

Before he returned to the Braves' rotation, Kevin pitched in the minor leagues. In his first appearance, he pitched three perfect innings. While Kevin was in the minors, several major league teams were keeping their eyes on his comeback progress. The Cincinnati Reds liked what they saw and wanted to make a trade with the Braves to get him. But the Braves still had plenty of confidence in Kevin and would not let him go.

Kevin returned to the Braves' rotation on July 20 in a losing effort against the Montreal Expos. But in his next two starts, he looked like the Kevin of old. After beating the Reds on July 25, Kevin expressed his satisfaction with his performance: "I never thought it [winning another game] would ever happen again," he said. "When I needed a good pitch, I was able to make it. Earlier in the year, I couldn't do that. . . . My job is to give us a chance to win, and today I did that," he added.

Kevin finished the 2001 season by going 7–7 with a 4.31 ERA.

Kevin has had lots of ups and downs on his comeback trail, but the Braves never gave up on Kevin. Most importantly, Kevin never gave up on himself.

>>SEAN CASEY

He's the definition of "a nice hitter"

Sean Casey is nice. *Really* nice. The Cincinnati Reds' All–Star first baseman always has a big smile on his face. When he meets a person for the first time, he shakes hands, and he makes sure that he remembers the person's name the next time they meet. People who know Sean say that he shakes more hands than a politician. That's why Sean's nickname is "The Mayor."

"I've always been taught to treat other people how I like to be treated," says Sean. "I know I like it when someone says, 'Hey, Case, how you doin'?' So when I walk by someone, I say hello."

Sean carries that attitude onto the field when he's

playing. After he reaches first base on a walk or a hit, he says hello to the other team's first baseman. And because he is so respectful, he calls the player "Mister" — as in "Mister McGwire," "Mister Bagwell," and "Mister Grace."

Mark Grace, the Arizona Diamondbacks first baseman, says he wishes that more young players had Sean's polite, cheery attitude. "He dropped a Mr. Grace on me one night at first base," says Mark. "I told him, 'You don't have to call me Mr. Grace. Mr. Grace is my father!'"

Sean's batting ability is every bit as nice as his sunny personality. He hit .332 in 1999, only his second full season in the major leagues. His average was the fourth-highest in the N.L. Sean rapped out 197 hits with 25 homers, 42 doubles, and 99 RBIs. He was only 25 years old, but he had already become one of the best hitters in baseball.

Very nice!

WELCOME TO THE MACHINE

Sean Casey was born on July 2, 1974, in Willingboro, New Jersey. He was kind of pudgy as a kid. "I was fat," he says with a laugh.

Sean wasn't a great hitter in Little League. His father, Jim, helped him develop his batting skills by buying a hitting machine while Sean was in high school. Sean set up the machine in the garage and spent hour after hour taking batting practice. The Casey family was living in Upper St. Clair, Pennsylvania, at the time.

Sean hit just .200 as a sophomore on the Upper St. Clair High School junior varsity team. The following season, his daily batting practice sessions began to pay off. Sean made the varsity team and banged out a sparkling .541 batting average. He was on his way to stardom.

Sean attended college at the University of Richmond, in Virginia, and earned a reputation as a great clutch hitter. During his junior season, in 1995, Sean needed a hit in his last at–bat of the season to capture the National Collegiate Athletic Association (NCAA) batting championship. He ignored the pressure and belted a double to win the crown with a whopping .461 average.

CLIMBING THE LADDER

The Cleveland Indians chose Sean in the second round of the major league draft a few days later. He decided to turn pro. During his first summer in the minors, Sean hit .329 and led the Watertown (New York) Indians to the 1995 New York–Penn League championship. The next season, Sean won the Carolina League batting title with a .331 average.

Sean kept climbing the ladder to the majors during 1997. He was hitting .386 for the Double-A Canton-Akron (Ohio) Aeros when he was promoted to Triple-A Buffalo (New York). At Buffalo, he hit .361 and earned his dream promotion — to the major leagues — on September 12.

statcity

SEAN CASEY

TEAM	Cincinnati Reds
POSITION	First baseman
ACQUIRED	Traded to the Reds by the Cleveland Indians for pitcher Dave Burba on March 30, 1998
BORN	July 2, 1974, in Willingboro, New Jersey
HEIGHT	6' 4"
WEIGHT	225 pounds
BATS	Left
THROWS	Right
BIG FEAT	Sean rapped five hits in six at-bats against the Kansas City Royals on June 6, 1999.
HONORS	N.L. All-Star, 2001, 1999

He pinch-hit in the ninth inning of the game that night and singled against the Chicago White Sox at Comiskey Park, in Chicago, Illinois.

"People always said that only one of every ten minor league players will reach the major leagues," says Sean. "I always said, 'Why not me? Why can't I be one of them?'"

Now he *was* one of them.

CINCINNATI SHOCKER

Sean was shocked the following March when the Indians traded him to the Reds for pitcher Dave Burba. Three days into the 1998 season, Sean had an even *more* shocking experience. During batting practice, teammate Damian Jackson accidentally hit Sean in the face with a throw. The infielders had been practicing double plays when Damian took a toss at second base from shortstop Barry Larkin, then fired a hard throw to first that took Sean by surprise, hitting him in the face.

Sean was seriously injured. The bone around his right eye was broken in four places. He needed 20 stitches to close the cut. He couldn't see out of his eye for two days.

Seeing the baseball well is the key to hitting well. Sean couldn't see at all. He was scared that his career might be over. But he kept his courage up and hoped for the best.

"I didn't want to get down on myself about it," he says. "I tried to keep a positive attitude and do what I had to do to get back on the field."

Sean's vision came back several days later, but his batting stroke needed more time to recover. Sean missed five weeks. When he returned to the Reds' lineup, he struggled, hitting only .135 in 16 games. The Reds decided to send Sean to the minor leagues for a while so he could regain his batting skills.

He spent a month there. He got his batting average up to .326 and drove in 14 runs in 27 games, then returned to Cincinnati on June 18. Back in the big leagues, he hit .300 during the second half of the season.

A HELPING HAND

After he came back from his horrible injury, Sean wanted to help others who faced similar problems. In the spring of 1999, a player for Evansville University named Anthony Molina was also hit in the face during practice. He suffered the same type of eye injury that Sean did. Sean called Anthony to cheer him up and give him some friendly advice.

"I talked to Anthony about how it was an awful thing that happened to him, but it was a situation in which you have to say, 'Where do I go from here?'" says Sean. "It was nice to be able to relate to him, raise his spirits a little bit, and tell him that things would be okay in the end."

Things were more than okay for Sean from the beginning of the 1999 season. He had three hits on Opening Day, against the San Francisco Giants, and three hits the next night. His bat stayed red hot for three months. Sean's best night was May 19, against the Colorado Rockies. He hit two homers and two singles, scored five runs, and had six RBIs in the Reds' 24–12 win!

By June 27, Sean was leading the N.L. with a .387 batting average. He was rewarded by making his first All-Star team. Sean was so excited about going to Boston's Fenway Park for the game that he taped the entire experience with his video camera. First, he even video-taped his plane ride from Cincinnati to Boston! The night of the game, Sean was shown on national TV taping his teammates in the National League dugout!

He batted twice in the game, grounding out and reaching first on a walk. The N.L. lost to the A.L., 6–1, but it was a night Sean will never forget.

CONFIDENCE MAN

What's the key to Sean's hitting success? One answer is his confidence. He believes he can get a hit off any pitcher, even Randy Johnson of the Arizona Diamondbacks. Randy is the most feared left-handed pitcher in the major leagues. Left-handed hitters hate to bat against Randy because he is so tall (6 feet 10 inches) and throws so hard. His overpowering fastball zooms in at 98 miles per hour, often right by the ribs or under the chin of a lefty batter.

Randy mows down lefty batters like a lawn mower cutting grass in the backyard! Even left-handed All-Star sluggers, such as Rafael Palmeiro of the Texas Rangers and Larry Walker of the Colorado Rockies, have decided to sit out games when Randy was pitching. But when the Reds faced Randy in a May 1999 game, Sean didn't want to take the day off, even though he bats lefty. In the bottom of the sixth inning, Sean drove one of Randy's fearsome fastballs into left field for a single.

"I've always felt I can hit at every level — and the big leagues shouldn't be any different," says Sean. "I think you have to rise to your level of competition."

Sean's sizzling bat drove the Reds through a thrilling 1999 season. They challenged the favored Houston Astros for the N.L. Central Division title all the way to the final day of the regular season in October. The Reds wound up playing the New York Mets in a one-game playoff to decide the National League wild-card playoff spot. Unfortunately for Sean and his teammates, they lost to the Mets, 5–0.

Sean struck out in the ninth inning. He was so upset that he broke his bat over his knee. Afterward, he cried in the clubhouse. It was one of the few times Sean was seen without his usual smile.

HIGH HOPES

Sean was anxious to find new reasons to smile as he and the Reds prepared for the 2000 season. The team believed that they could go even further in the playoffs because they had just acquired superstar centerfielder Ken Griffey, Jr. from the Seattle Mariners. With Ken's big bat in the lineup, expectations were huge.

But in the last exhibition game of the preseason, Sean broke his right thumb and was placed on the 15–day disabled list. He missed the Reds' first 14 games of the regular season. After his return to the lineup, Sean had

Sean Casey

Sean's hitting skills often overshadow his fine glovework.

Hall of Fame DOUBLE

George Kelly hit .303 or higher six seasons in a row with the New York Giants (1921 to 1926). He had a .297 career batting average. Like Sean, George wasn't a slugger. He sprayed line drives all over the field. He was nicknamed "Highpockets" because he was very tall for players of the early 20th century. He stood 6 feet 4 inches, just like Sean, and was known for being very friendly, just like Sean! George was elected to the Hall of Fame in 1973.

trouble finding his groove. By late May he was batting only .221 and he wasn't showing the power he displayed in his All-Star season.

Still, he managed to keep the positive outlook that made him one of the National League's biggest threats in 1999. "I'm out there battling and I'm going to keep battling. I'm going to have a great season. That's the bottom line," he said.

CASEY AT THE BAT

Ultimately, Sean was right — he did have a great season. From the beginning of July to the end of the season, he was unstoppable. He batted .369 in July, .349 in August, and .378 in September and October. He was the hottest hitter in the N.L. after the All–Star break, batting .372.

Sean even notched a career–high 21–game hitting streak in which he batted .403 with four home runs and 17 RBIs. He finished the season with five home runs and 15 RBIs in the last eight games, including the last home run ever hit at Milwaukee's County Stadium, before it was torn down.

Despite playing in only 133 games, Sean finished the season with 20 homers, 85 RBIs, 151 hits, and a .315 batting average. Sean was back — and as dangerous as ever.

But even with the addition of Ken Griffey, Jr. to the lineup, and Sean's successful second–half comeback, the Reds failed to make it to the playoffs in 2000. They won 11 fewer games than they did in 1999, finishing with an 85–77 record.

REACHING FOR THE STARS

The Reds were hoping for a quick start in 2001 and Sean helped provide them with the spark they needed. Playing in the Pittsburgh Pirates' brand–new PNC Park, Sean unloaded on a Todd Ritchie fastball and crushed the first hit and home run ever at the new ballpark. His heroics were just a warm-up for the weeks to follow.

On June 22, with last season's hitting woes far behind him, Sean faced the Astros' star reliever Billy Wagner in the tenth inning of a tied ballgame. Sean had never had a hit against the flamethrowing right-hander in four career at-bats, but tonight was different. He lashed an RBI single, driving in the go-ahead run and leading the Reds to a 7-5 come-from-behind win.

Sean stayed hot through the first half of the season and was chosen to the N.L. All-Star team. He was the only player from the Reds given the honor. "One of my goals was to try to get back to the All-Star Game," Sean said. It was a personal goal that he didn't share with many others. "Probably the only person I told was my wife," he added.

Sean's rise as one of baseball's most dependable hitters has gained him plenty of attention. Houston Astro Jeff Bagwell has a lot of respect for Sean's talents. "'Case' is the kind of guy who might not hit thirty or forty home runs right now, but he's getting that two-run single when the team needs it. That's all that matters — getting guys across the plate," he said.

In 2001, Sean continued to get guys across the plate as he knocked in 89 runs to go along with a .310 average.

Even with another All–Star selection under his belt, Sean had looked to improve his game. "I'm having a pretty good start, but I'm not satisfied. I don't think I'll ever be. That's the one thing that drives me every day. You can always do better," he said.

And if Sean does find away to get any better, all you can say to opposing National League pitchers is: "Watch out!"

It doesn't matter who is pitching. The scene is usually the same: Sean banging out another base hit.

>>NOMAR GARCIAPARRA

His name is unforgettable. So is the way he plays.

Former Boston Red Sox manager Jimy Williams says that shortstop Nomar Garciaparra reminds him of the stars who played in the major leagues 50 years ago. Those great players hustled on every play and made sure they knew the fundamentals of the game. They did the little things that can help a team win, such as running hard to first base after hitting the ball, bunting runners into scoring position, and steal–ing bases. Those players tried hard *all the time*. Nomar plays the same way.

"He plays like he's been here before," says Jimy.

Actually, Nomar only joined the major leagues in

NOMAR GARCIAPARRA

TEAM	Boston Red Sox
POSITION	Shortstop
ACQUIRED	Chosen by the Red Sox in the first round (12th player chosen overall) of the major league draft on June 2, 1994
BORN	July 23, 1973, in Whittier, California
HEIGHT	6'
WEIGHT	180 pounds
BATS	Right
THROWS	Right
BIG FEATS	Nomar won back-to-back A.L. batting titles in 1999 and 2000. He also hit three home runs and had 10 RBIs in a game against the Seattle Mariners on May 10, 1999.
HONORS	A.L. All-Star, 2000, 1999, 1997; A.L. Silver Slugger Award, 1997; A.L. Rookie of the Year, 1997

1997. He was chosen as the A.L. Rookie of the Year that season. Now, he's putting up better numbers than your math teacher.

In 1998, Nomar hit .323 with 35 homers and 122 RBIs. He finished second to then-Texas Ranger slugger Juan Gonzalez in the voting for the A.L. MVP award. In 1999,

Nomar played in his second All-Star Game and won the American League batting title with a .357 average. He powered the BoSox into the A.L. Championship Series.

Texas Ranger catcher Ivan Rodriguez was named the 1999 A.L. Most Valuable Player, but Nomar will surely win the MVP award one day. Just don't talk to him about awards and stats. Like a true old-time star, he doesn't like to think about that stuff. He wants to focus on his team.

"Did we win or lose? That's what interests me," says Nomar. "My job is to play hard and do the best I can. I don't think I'm better than anybody else."

Many baseball fans think Nomar is better than Derek Jeter of the New York Yankees and Alex Rodriguez of the Texas Rangers, the other young superstar shortstops. Even Derek and Alex are Nomar fans.

"Nomar brings a lot of energy. I like the way he plays," says Alex. Adds Derek: "Nomar goes out and plays hard. He's always a threat to do something big."

THE NAME GAME

The boy who would one day be a big-league superstar was born on July 23, 1973, in Whittier, California. His father, Ramon Garciaparra, wanted his son to have a unique name. Mr. Garciaparra chose the name "Nomar," which was his own name (Ramon) spelled backward.

"He's going to make the name famous!" Ramon proudly told Nomar's mother, Sylvia.

Famous or not, Mrs. Garciaparra wanted her son to have a more normal name. She insisted on "Anthony Nomar Garciaparra." And so it is. But it didn't take long for young Anthony to prefer his *middle* name. "When somebody yells out 'Nomar!' you don't have to worry about five people answering!" he says.

NO-NONSENSE NOMAR

As a kid, Nomar liked to play soccer. But he loved baseball. When he was a 6-year-old in tee ball, Nomar took baseball so seriously that the parents of his team-mates nicknamed him "No-nonsense Nomar." He was always eager to practice and learn.

"I'd tell my dad, 'Don't tell me about who plays the game in the majors. Tell me *how* to play it,'" Nomar says. "I wanted to learn as much as I could about every position."

Sometimes, Nomar took baseball too seriously. He had a bad temper and often threw his glove or his batting helmet after he made bad plays or struck out.

Mr. Garciaparra hated to see his son act so poorly. He often told Nomar, "You're not always the best player. Just go out there and try to do your best."

In time, Nomar took his dad's advice to heart. "I began to understand in high school that getting mad wasn't helping me," Nomar says. "There is no need to show that kind of emotion. It rubs off on your teammates."

Nomar made the varsity team at St. John Bosco High School. His solid play at shortstop attracted scouts from major league teams. One scout told Nomar that he could make his hands quicker and surer by throwing a ball against a wall and fielding the rebound. Nomar began fielding 100 throws a day off a wall near his house. That helped him develop what many baseball experts say are the quickest hands — at bat and in the field — in the majors.

Nomar led his high school team to league champion- ships in 1990 and 1991. He was his league's MVP in 1991. The Milwaukee Brewers chose him in the fifth round of the major league draft that year. He also received several scholarship offers from major colleges.

Nomar decided to attend Georgia Tech University so that he could study business management while he continued to improve his baseball skills. He wanted to have an education to fall back on, just in case he didn't make it to the major leagues. Nomar figured that anoth- er team would draft him later if he played well for Georgia Tech's team.

Sure enough, Nomar was drafted again. The Red Sox chose him in the first round of the 1994 draft, after he hit .427 with 16 homers during his junior season. Nomar decided to leave school and become a pro baseball player.

TURNING ON THE POWER

Nomar wasn't a slugger when he began his pro career in the minor leagues. He developed his power accidentally while he was playing for Triple-A Pawtucket (Rhode Island) in 1996.

While running to first base during a game that season, Nomar tore a tendon in his left knee. He couldn't play for three months. When he came back, he discovered that he could hit the ball farther than he used to. He had done so much weightlifting during his recovery that he had bulked up from 165 to 180 pounds. The extra weight was muscle, and that gave him extra power. Nomar blasted 13 homers in his next 40 games for Pawtucket.

Next, Nomar blasted himself right into the majors.

WINNING FRIENDS

Nomar began the 1997 season with the Red Sox. It was an uncomfortable time. When Nomar made the team, veteran shortstop John Valentin had to move to second base. Second baseman Jeff Frye was benched. Both players resented Nomar at first, but he earned their friendship with his quiet, respectful attitude.

"He's a nice kid," John Valentin told reporters. "What I like about Nomar is that he listens. He asks you questions, and he learns."

Nomar Garciaparra

Nomar has been dazzling BoSox fans since he joined the team in 1996.

Hall of Fame DOUBLE

Ernie Banks was a great power-hitting shortstop. Nicknamed "Mr. Cub," he played for the Chicago Cubs from 1953 to 1971, and hit 512 career homers. He was a great fielder before injuries forced him to move to first base. Like Nomar, Ernie loved baseball. He would say, "It's a beautiful day for baseball. Let's play two!" Ernie never played in a World Series. (Nomar hopes to do better!) Ernie was elected to the Hall of Fame in 1977.

Nomar had one of the best seasons ever by a rookie shortstop. He hit .306 and walloped 30 home runs, a major league record for a rookie shortstop. He also had 98 RBIs, which was the most ever by a leadoff hitter. He led the league with 209 hits and 11 triples. He led the Red Sox with 22 stolen bases. He had a 30–game hitting streak, the longest ever by an American League rookie.

On top of that, Nomar played outstanding defense. He

made so many great defensive plays that teammate Mo Vaughn (who left the Red Sox to join the Anaheim Angels in 1999) nicknamed him "Spider-Man." Said Mo: "He's so quick, and sometimes it seems like he can suspend himself in midair."

"He's fun to watch, isn't he?" added former Red Sox manager Jimy Williams.

Nomar's sparkling season made him the first Red Sox player since 1975 to win the A.L. Rookie of the Year award. People assumed that Nomar was surprised by his amazing season. He wasn't. "When you're surprised, it's because you've gone over your goals," says Nomar. "I never set goals, so I can't say I've gone over what I expected."

One thing Nomar does expect is good luck.

FEAR OF A CLEAN HAT

Nomar is one of the most superstitious players in the majors. The list of quirky things he does to ward off bad luck is longer than a black cat's tail:

- Nomar never replaces or washes his hat.
- He wears the same T-shirt every day until it's so torn and tattered that it no longer stays on his body.
- Before he steps into the batter's box, he pulls hard at his batting gloves, six, seven, or eight times. (He likes to make sure they're nice and snug.)
- After he steps into the box, he always taps his toes with his bat.

- He always enters the dugout one step at a time, putting both feet on each step as he goes.

"I am superstitious, but I like to be in a routine so that I feel comfortable out there," says Nomar.

Nomar must have felt very comfortable in 1999. He gave the Red Sox a thrilling ride all season and into the playoffs. He hit .417 and belted two homers as the Red Sox upset the favored Cleveland Indians, three games to two, in the A.L. Division Series. In the ALCS, against the Yankees, Nomar hit .400 with two more homers. Twice in Game 1, he saved runs with great, leaping catches of line drives. Still, the Yankees beat the Red Sox, four games to one. Then the Yankees went on to sweep the Atlanta Braves in the World Series.

Although the ALCS loss was a disappointment for Nomar, he had once again shown that he was one of baseball's top clutch players.

MILLENNIUM MAN

The 2000 season got underway and Nomar picked up where he left off in 1999. Despite a leg injury in May that put him on the 15-day disabled list, Nomar was batting .389 by the All-Star break. Not surprisingly, he made the A.L. All-Star team for the third time.

The highlights kept coming. On July 17, Nomar raised his average above .400. He was the first hitter to be above .400 that late in a season since Colorado Rockie

Larry Walker in 1997. No one had batted .400 in a season since Ted Williams hit .406 in 1941. A few days later, Nomar hit the 10,000th home run in Red Sox history in an interleague game against the Montreal Expos.

Pitchers respected Nomar's hot bat and they pitched around him whenever they could. Because of that, Nomar ended up leading the league with 20 intentional walks. When they did pitch to him, Nomar made A.L. pitchers pay dearly. He ended the season with a .372 batting average, walking off with his second consecutive batting title. He finished fifth in the league in hits (197) and second in doubles (51).

Nomar downplayed his fine 2000 season in typical style: "Numbers are irrelevant to me . . . all I care about is wins and losses," he said.

Unfortunately, the Red Sox didn't pick up enough wins in 2000, finishing at 85–77. They failed to make the playoffs. All they could do was wait out the cold New England winter and hope for a World Series championship in 2001— something they had not accomplished since 1918!

NO MORE NOMAR

Preparations for the Red Sox 2001 championship run began in spring training at the Red Sox camp in Fort Myers, Florida. However, the team was dealt bad news when it was learned that a wrist injury would sideline

Nomar for at least two weeks. Nomar and his doctor believed the injury originally happened back in September 1999 when Nomar was hit on the wrist with a pitch. His wrist had bothered him ever since.

The bad news got worse. Nomar's wrist didn't heal enough for a spring training return, and on Opening Day of the 2001 season, Nomar underwent surgery. The recovery process kept him out of the Red Sox lineup for 17 weeks of the season. Amazingly, the Red Sox played extremely well without their star shortstop, battling the Yankees for first place in the A.L Eastern Division.

When Nomar did return on July 29, his performance put everyone on notice that the two-time batting champ was back — and as clutch a hitter as ever. Nomar hit a game-tying home run and then added a bases-loaded single late in the game to lead the Red Sox to a 4-3 win over the Chicago White Sox.

Nomar was delighted to be part of the team again. "I definitely missed it. I love playing the game. It puts a smile on my face," he said.

Boston eventually fell out of the pennant race and Nomar was given lots of rest. He finished the season with four home runs, eight RBIs, and a .289 batting average.

Nomar should be back in top form in 2002 — and luck will have nothing to do with it.

At bat or in the field, Nomar is as intense as
anyone in the major leagues.

>> JASON KENDALL

Hard-nosed, hustling Jason is a total "dirt dog"

When he isn't playing catcher for the Pittsburgh Pirates, Jason Kendall is a very laid-back guy. He can spend hours on his sofa, watching movies and pro wrestling on television. He loves to go to the beach and surf the waves of the Pacific Ocean.

"Off the field, I can be the most boring person you'll ever meet," says Jason. "But when I'm playing, it's like I turn on a light switch — I'm a different person. Instincts take over. I'm gonna do whatever I can to beat you."

That's bad news for the poor person who has to wash the Pirates' laundry after their games. Jason

plays so hard that his uniform is always filthy. It's soaked with sweat and covered with dirt from blocking pitches and sliding runners at home plate or from diving into bases after he's banged out another hit.

Jason is a total dirt dog whenever he's on the field. He takes his job so seriously that he dreams about the game at night. Jason even talks about baseball in his sleep. He might blurt out "curveball" or "change-up," as if he were calling pitches during a game. One night, Jason dreamed he was hitting a home run, and he screamed, *"It's outta here!"*

TOTAL INTENSITY

Jason's intensity has helped him become the best young catcher in baseball. In 1998, he played in his second All-Star Game right after he had turned 24. Through 2001, after six full seasons with the Pirates, he had a .304 career batting average.

Jason has surprising speed for a catcher, too. He steals about 25 bases each season. To top it off, he is also tougher than a concrete hamburger. While batting, he was hit by pitches 89 times in his first four seasons.

Here's a typical Jason moment: The Pirates were playing the San Diego Padres on April 24, 1998. Jason was zooming down the third-base line trying to score when he realized that Padre catcher Carlos Hernandez had the ball. So Jason jumped over Carlos and brushed the plate with his hand as he crash–landed in a cloud of dust: Safe!

"He was like a gymnast," said Gene Lamont, then Pirate manager.

Toronto Blue Jay pitcher Esteban Loaiza, a former Pirate, says Jason is like a cat. "He takes his claws out," says Esteban, "and gives you everything he's got."

THE CATCHER'S SON

Jason was born on June 26, 1974, in San Diego, California. He comes from a baseball family. His father, Fred, was a major league catcher from 1969 to 1980. Fred Kendall spent most of his career with the Padres. He had a reputation as a terrific team leader.

Fred and his wife, Patty, had two sons: Mike and Jason. The Kendalls lived near San Diego, in the small city of Torrance. When Fred played for the Padres, Mrs. Kendall, Jason, and Mike often went to Jack Murphy Stadium (now Qualcomm Park) to watch him. But Jason and Mike had so much energy they couldn't sit still. They played little baseball games against a wall in the grandstand. Sometimes, the brothers got so wrapped up in *their* games that they missed seeing their dad take his turn at bat!

Jason loved to play catch with his dad. But Mr. Kendall was often on road trips with the Padres during the summer. So Jason played with his mom, instead. Mrs. Kendall

67

JASON KENDALL

TEAM	Pittsburgh Pirates
POSITION	Catcher
ACQUIRED	Chosen by the Pirates in the first round (the 23rd player chosen overall) of the major league draft on June 1, 1992
BORN	June 26, 1974, in San Diego, California
HEIGHT	6'
WEIGHT	193 pounds
BATS	Right
THROWS	Right
BIG FEAT	Jason set the N.L. single-season record for most stolen bases by a catcher in 1998. He stole 26 bases.
HONORS	N.L. All-Star, 2000, 1998, 1996

found that she really enjoyed teaching Jason, so she became his first tee–ball coach.

"She'd go out there and pound ground balls at me when my dad was away," says Jason. "Even today, if I want to throw and my dad's not there, I'll get my mom."

When Jason was seven and old enough to play Little League, his dad saw that Jason had his baseball talent. "I was amazed and impressed," said Mr. Kendall. "He just stood out. You could see the talent, the strength, and the ability. He's just an incredible athlete."

Jason wanted to follow in his dad's footsteps and become a catcher. He didn't like playing other positions, anyway. He was bored when he played the outfield because the ball was rarely hit to him. Jason wanted to be involved with every pitch and every play.

Jason learned the fundamentals of playing catcher from his dad. He worked on improving his skills by having his brother, Mike, pitch to him every day. By the time Jason was a senior at Torrance High School, in 1992, he had become one of the best baseball prospects in the United States. He hit a whopping .549 that season! He also tied the national high school record by getting hit by a pitch in 43 consecutive games.

YOUNG BUC

The Pirates chose Jason in the first round of the 1992 major league draft. He started off slowly in his minor league career, batting only .252 with no homers and 10 RBIs in 33 games for the Gulf Coast League Pirates. Jason stayed with it, and he finally began to blossom in 1995. He hit .326 that season for the Carolina Mudcats and was named MVP of the Double–A Southern League.

The Pirates were so impressed that they decided to

make Jason their Opening Day catcher in 1996. He went three-for-four, with two RBIs, against the Florida Marlins that day. He even smacked a single off ace pitcher Kevin Brown. It quickly became a dream season for Jason. He smashed his first major league homer on May 8 against the Padres and played in his first All-Star Game. He hit .300 for the season and finished third in the voting for the 1996 National League Rookie of the Year award.

"I didn't want to start slow," says Jason. "I didn't want to waste time establishing myself in the majors."

LEADING THE CREW

Jason played so hard and so well that he became the leader of the Pirates even though he was one of the younger guys. He led by example, stealing bases, making tough plays behind the plate, and getting his uniform dirty. He also had sharp words for his teammates if he saw them being lazy.

"If something needs to be said, I'm not scared to say it," Jason says. "But I like to be a team player. I hope that people can watch me and want to play the game the way I play it — running out ground balls, breaking up double plays. That's how I want to be a team leader."

Jason also became one of the best base-stealing catchers in major league history. He swiped 26 bags in

Jason Kendall

Playing catcher is a rough, tough, dirty job — one that's just for Jason.

Hall of Fame DOUBLE

Mickey Cochrane was one of the fiercest competitors baseball has ever known. He was a catcher for the Philadelphia Athletics and Detroit Tigers from 1925 to 1937. He batted .320, the highest career average ever for a catcher who played 10 seasons or more. Like Jason, Mickey was a fast baserunner. He occasionally batted leadoff. A great leader, Mickey later became the Tigers' manager. He was elected to the Hall of Fame in 1947.

1998 to set the National League record for most steals in one season by a catcher. Jason also hit .327 that season, which ranked fifth in the league. He cracked 12 homers, drove in 75 runs, and led the Pirates in runs scored (95). Behind the plate, Jason led all N.L. catchers with 1,015 putouts while making only nine errors. And he was an All-Star, too!

MAJOR LEAGUE ACHES AND PAINS

Jason doesn't mind the pain that comes with playing hard. But one injury he suffered during the 1999 season was horrifying for him and everyone who saw it happen. On July 4, against the Milwaukee Brewers, Jason bunted and was running hard to first base when he stepped awkwardly on the bag. He took a couple more steps and then suddenly collapsed in terrible pain. Jason had fractured and dislocated his right ankle. His foot hung off the end of his leg like a twisted rag.

"It hurt pretty bad," says Jason. "Worse than you can ever imagine."

Pirate manager at the time, Gene Lamont, was so upset that he almost cried in the clubhouse after the game. "Jason is the heart and soul of this team," said Gene.

The gruesome injury caused Jason to miss the rest of the season. Before he was hurt, Jason had been off to another hot start, batting .332 in 78 games. But he didn't get too down about the injury.

"I'm dealing with it," he told reporters. "What choice do you have? What choice does anyone have when they have problems in their life?"

THE COMEBACK

Jason was determined to come back to the Pirates and play as he always has — with 100 percent effort. He spent the offseason pushing himself through a daily workout routine that lasted from 8:30 A.M. to 5 P.M.

"I won't ever bunt again," he joked to reporters. "I'm not worried about being as good as I was before I got hurt."

The previous time Jason suffered a nasty injury, it didn't turn out so bad. The injury happened when he was in eighth grade. During a winter trip to the mountains, he rode his toboggan into a tree and broke his leg. Jason's doctor said swimming would help strengthen the leg. So once he got the cast off his leg, Jason did a lot of swimming in the Pacific Ocean. It was during that time that he discovered surfing.

"It relaxes me," says Jason. "I just ride the waves and let the sun go down. When you go out on a wave, you don't think about baseball. You're really in a different world."

BACK IN THE GROOVE

Jason immediately got back to the real world — rehabilitating his ankle and getting ready to play in 2000. His recovery was a long–term process that took a lot of effort. "I know how hard I worked during the off–season. Nobody else does. It was a nine–to–five job every day for months," he said.

But once he got back into playing form, Jason was raring to go. He opened the season by batting .322 in April and a sizzling .379 in May. His fast start earned him a spot on the N.L. All-Star team — the third time he was selected.

Jason finished the season batting .320 with 58 RBIs and career highs of 14 home runs and 185 hits. He led the Pirates in batting average, at bats, runs, hits and stolen bases. With his 22 thefts, he became the first catcher in major league baseball history to steal 20 or more bases in three seasons.

On September 14, as Jason's successful comeback season was winding down, he was hit in the face on a pick-off throw by Houston Astros pitcher Chris Holt. The throw fractured Jason's right cheekbone. He had surgery to repair the damage on October 2. It was a painful conclusion to Jason's solid season.

In November 2000, Jason signed a new six-year, $60 million contract with the Pirates. Jason had a strong desire to continue playing in Pittsburgh. "I wouldn't have signed here for six more years if I didn't think we [could] win a world championship here. I want to win here. I want to get a ring here. And when I get that ring, I'm going to put it under my pillow and try to get another the next year," he said.

OPENING DAY HEROICS

The first game ever played at PNC Park was on Opening Day, April 9, 2001. It was fitting that Jason got the Pirates' first hit ever at their new stadium with a first-inning single off Cincinnati Red pitcher Chris Reitsma. "This is our new home and nobody could be happier [than me]. This is the most beautiful ballpark in the game," he said.

ROAMING THE OUTFIELD

Since his rookie season in 1996, Jason had been averaging about 123 starts behind the plate as a catcher. That's a lot of time playing the most physically-challenging position on the field — especially for someone like Jason who's not afraid to take his lumps. In an effort to get Jason more rest and to get his bat in the lineup more often, manager Lloyd McClendon started to occasionally play Jason in the outfield in 2001.

Jason likes the idea of the move to the outfield. "It's a way for me to take a day off from catching without having to take a day off altogether. I hate days off, but I also realize you're not going to be able to catch all one-hundred-sixty-two games in a season. This way, I can get rest for my legs and still have the chance to play," he says.

On May 25, against the Atlanta Braves, Jason made his debut in left field — making a spectacular sliding catch of a Quilvio Veras flyball. Jason had brought the same rough–and–tumble attitude to the outfield that he's always had behind the plate. And he was having fun, too.

"I actually enjoyed my first time out there," he said. "It's a lot less stressful and much more relaxing than [playing] catcher. You don't have to stand there all night and worry about the hitters [or] think about how we got them out last time and how we'll get them out this time."

By early August, Jason was struggling, batting just .251 with seven home runs and 42 RBIs in 108 games. Jason is intensely wrapped up in his on–field performances, often waking up in the middle of the night thinking about an at–bat.

He finished the year by batting a career–low .266 with 10 home runs and 53 RBIs. But quitting is not a way of life for Jason, who knows that slumps are a part of base-ball life — even for All–Star players. "I'll keep plugging away. That's all there is to do. I can't sit here and go home and pout and cry. I've just got to go out and do whatever I can to help the team win," he said.

This gritty dirt dog is going to do anything and every-thing he can to get back on top of his game.

>>BILLY WAGNER

The ace Astro closer throws unbeatable heat

When pitcher Billy Wagner trots in from the bullpen and starts firing fastballs, even the mightiest sluggers often look as if they were swinging tooth-picks instead of bats. Billy is the ace closer of the Houston Astros. He is the hardest-throwing left-handed pitcher in the major leagues. His fastball has been timed at a sizzling 100 miles per hour!

"It's sick," moans All-Star slugger Larry Walker of the Colorado Rockies. "Billy can make you look completely stupid."

Even Slammin' Sammy Sosa of the Chicago Cubs struggles to hit Billy's fiery heater. Sammy struck out

six times in his first seven career at–bats against Billy. "I love throwing the ball as hard as I can," says Billy. "I just say to the batter, 'Here it is . . . try to hit it.'"

They usually can't.

No one whiffs hitters more often than Billy. In 1998, he broke the major league record by averaging 14.6 strikeouts for every nine innings he pitched. Whose record did he break? His own! Billy set the record for most strikeouts per nine innings three seasons in a row. The 1998 season was only Billy's third in the majors, but he had already become one of the best strikeout artists in baseball history.

Billy is also one of the best closers in the major leagues. He saved 30 games for the Astros in 1998 and 39 in 1999. The Astros finished first in the N.L. Central Division both seasons. In 1999, Billy's earned run average was a puny 1.57, and batters hit just .135 against him. Both of those numbers were the lowest in the majors among pitchers who threw at least 50 innings.

What's really amazing about Billy is that he throws so hard even though he isn't a big guy. He is one of the shortest pitchers in the majors — just 5 feet 11 inches — and he weighs only 180 pounds. Some of his teammates call him "Wee Willy Billy." People have even mistaken Billy for the Astro batboy!

A SELF-MADE LEFTY

Billy hasn't always been a hard-throwing lefty. Would you believe that he once threw righty?

Billy was born July 25, 1971, in Tannersville, Virginia. He first learned to throw right-handed. But when he was three, he broke his right arm while playing in his grandmother's yard. He had to wear a cast on his arm for six months.

Billy couldn't stand not throwing for that long, so he started to throw with his *left* arm. He still brushes his teeth, uses a fork, and writes with his right hand. He just never stopped throwing left-handed.

Billy had a troubled childhood, and that had nothing to do with his broken arm. Billy's hometown, Tannersville, was a tiny farming community near the Appalachian mountains in Virginia. About 300 people live in Tannersville. It is so small that it has only one store!

Billy's parents, William and Yvonne Wagner, were poor. They struggled to provide him with enough food, clothing, and attention. Mr. and Mrs. Wagner were divorced when Billy was five years old. As a result, Billy moved from home to home. Sometimes he lived with his mom, sometimes with his dad. Sometimes he lived with either of his two sets of grandparents. But wherever Billy lived, the family he lived with was poor.

▶ BILLY WAGNER

TEAM	Houston Astros
POSITION	Pitcher
ACQUIRED	Chosen by the Astros in the first round (12th player chosen overall) of the major league draft on June 3, 1993
BORN	July 25, 1971, in Tannersville, Virginia
HEIGHT	5' 11"
WEIGHT	180 pounds
BATS	Left
THROWS	Left
BIG FEATS	Billy struck out the side 40 times in his first three full seasons. In 1999, he set an Astro team record for most saves in one season with 39. In 2001, he repeated the feat.
HONORS	N.L. All-Star, 2001, 1999; N.L. Rolaids Relief Award, 1999

GOING IT ALONE

Billy was a lonely kid. It was hard for him to make friends because he kept moving to different towns and attending different elementary schools. He often had no one to play catch with. So he went to the baseball field by himself each day. He threw the ball as hard and far as he could. Then he ran to where the ball had landed and picked it up. He threw it again. All that throwing helped Billy develop a strong arm.

Billy bounced around from family to family until he was 14. Then his aunt and uncle, Sally and Jeff Lamie, offered to let him live with them in Tannersville. "The Lamies were so important for me," says Billy. "They taught me discipline and made school important. Things started going my way."

BIRTH OF A FASTBALL

After he moved in with his aunt and uncle, Billy had to ride a bus for an hour each way to high school in Tazewell, Virginia. Many nights, he only slept from 3:00 A.M. to 6:00 A.M. because of schoolwork and sports practices. Billy loved playing football and baseball. But school was more important to Mr. and Mrs. Lamie. One day, Billy got a D in earth science. His aunt and uncle punished him by not letting him play in the state championship football game.

A major league baseball career seemed like a long shot when Billy was a teenager. For one thing, he was small — 5 feet 3 inches and 135 pounds. Pro scouts thought Billy wouldn't be big enough to play in the majors. Another problem was that he threw only 84 miles per hour when he was a senior in high school. Most coaches at colleges with strong baseball programs thought that

that wasn't good enough. So Billy ended up attending a small school in Virginia, called Ferrum College.

Billy's life changed in a big way during the next two years. He grew seven inches and gained 40 pounds. Suddenly, he could make his fastball explode across the plate. He began throwing 98 miles per hour and became one of the best college pitchers in America.

Billy's stats at Ferrum College were amazing. He struck out 85 batters in only 56 innings as a freshman. He pitched a no-hitter against the State University of New York (SUNY) at Oneonta. As a sophomore, Billy set a Division III college record by fanning 109 batters in only 51 innings. That's more than two strikeouts per inning! He allowed only nine hits that entire season! Pro scouts started coming *by the dozens* to watch him play.

BLASTING OFF TO HOUSTON

In June 1993, the Houston Astros chose Billy in the first round of the major league draft. He was 21 years old and brimming with excitement and confidence. Early in his minor league career, Billy told a friend, "I can't wait to get to the majors and throw fastballs past Barry Bonds." (Barry is a ten-time All-Star slugger for the San Francisco Giants.)

Billy soon got his wish. He spent only three years in the minors. He was called up to Houston in June 1996. Sure enough, when the Astros faced the San Francisco

Giants in August, Billy took the mound against Barry Bonds. What did he do? He struck out Barry on three straight fastballs! Then, Billy did the same to Matt Williams, another All–Star slugger. Billy was ready for success in the major leagues.

Billy became the Astros' top reliever in 1997, when he saved 23 games. Then, in 1998, he survived a scary incident that nearly ended his career.

Pitching against the Arizona Diamondbacks on July 16, Billy was hit by a wicked line drive off the bat of Arizona's Kelly Stinnett. The ball hit Billy in the head hard. He went down. His teammates rushed to the mound. The fans in the ballpark became very quiet.

Billy was almost knocked out. He spent a night in the hospital and three weeks on the disabled list. It could have been a lot worse. Some pitchers would have been afraid to get back on the mound after a moment like that. But Billy wasn't fazed by what had happened to him. He had faced tough times and pain before.

"It never bothered me that I could have gotten killed," he says. "It's just something else I'll go through."

NO FEAR

Billy decided not to be afraid that he might get hit again. He wanted hitters to be afraid of him. They certainly should be. No pitcher has a fastball that's harder to hit than Billy's. His nasty slider makes him even tougher. Billy may be short, but he's long on talent.

He also has a long memory. Billy never forgets a bad game. If he pitches poorly, he tries twice as hard the next time he enters a game. In 1998, Billy gave up two home runs to the New York Mets and lost the game. He made sure he got revenge the next time he faced New York. In a game on May 5, 1999, Billy whiffed all four Met batters he faced to end the game and get the save.

"You make me look stupid, I'll get back at you," he says. "I'll get you somehow. All I want to do is strike you out."

After he set strikeout records three years in a row, Billy didn't relax. He knew that he had to keep trying to improve — or else another pitcher might beat him!

"If somebody like me can break the record, you know it can be broken again," says Billy. "Say I set the record at eighteen strikeouts per nine innings someday. I really believe that somebody can come out there in a couple of years and strike out nineteen."

Did Billy really think he could strike out 18 batters every nine innings? It seems impossible because he would have to fan 18 of every 27 hitters he retired! But Billy remembers the tough times he faced early in his life and how he surprised many people by reaching the major leagues.

Billy's not a big guy, but he throws an overpowering fastball.

Hall of Fame DOUBLE

Sandy Koufax was one of the best strikeout pitchers of all time. He pitched for the Brooklyn and Los Angeles Dodgers from 1955 to 1966. He led the National League in strikeouts in 1961, 1963, 1965, and 1966. His 382 whiffs in 1965 are the N.L. single-season record. He wasn't a reliever, but he was a lefty, like Billy. "I met Sandy," says Billy. "I was so excited, I didn't know what to say!" Sandy was elected to the Hall of Fame in 1971.

WHAT A RELIEF!

Billy's fierce determination and competitive spirit were never in evidence more than in the 1999 season. He appeared in 66 games with the Astros, converting 39 of 42 save opportunities. His 39 saves set a club record, as he went 4–1. His performance helped the Astros take first place in the N.L. Central Division for the third straight season. Billy's total domination of National League hitters was clearly shown as he posted more saves than hits allowed (35).

Billy's heroics earned him a spot on the National League All-Star team and he was named the N.L. Rolaids Relief Award winner — the honor given to the best relief pitcher in the league. He was the first Astro pitcher ever to win the award.

BLAME IT ON THE PAIN

Most pitchers, especially those who throw as hard as Billy, experience pain or discomfort in their arms or shoulders at some time during their careers. For Billy, it was the 2000 season — and his pain was unbearable.

After saving three of the Astros' first four wins of the season, Billy began to struggle on the mound. He blew nine of 15 save opportunities through late June and lost his closer's job to Octavio Dotel. In late June, he under-went season-ending surgery to repair a torn tendon in his left elbow.

The pain Billy was experiencing was not a secret in the Astros' clubhouse. "We knew he was hurting a little bit," said second baseman Craig Biggio. "But he's such a professional that he's not going to say anything. He's going to try to pitch through it."

Billy took his poor 2000 performance very hard. "I'll be honest, when I'm out there at the start of last season blowing eight or nine saves in a row, I began to doubt myself," he said at the beginning of the 2001 season.

"It's natural. I wondered, 'Did I lose it in one year?'"

Billy's absence from the Astros' bullpen in the last 3½ months of the season ruined the team's chance of securing a playoff berth. The 'Stros sank to a 72–90 record and fourth place in the N.L. Central after three consecutive playoff appearances. Billy appeared in only 28 games, finishing 2–4 with a 6.18 ERA and only six saves — the poorest performance of his brilliant career.

Off-season rehabilitation was definitely in order.

BACK IN THE GROOVE

After time to rest and heal from the surgery, Billy had an outstanding spring training in preparation for the 2001 season. As soon as he took the mound in the regular season, it was clear that he was in top form again. His blazing fastball was being clocked at 94 to 96 miles per hour. Billy was back.

By early August, he had converted 25 of 27 save opportunities, including 16 in a row. It was no surprise that the Astros were in contention for a playoff spot, battling the Chicago Cubs for the N.L. Central's top spot.

Billy was selected to the 2001 National League All-Star team. Making the team meant a lot to the intimidating closer who had proven that he had successfully overcome his career-threatening surgery. "You just don't expect it [the All-Star selection]. You just want to stay healthy and pitch. All of a sudden, you're getting a call to tell you that you're an All-Star. What a great honor," he said.

Astros' manager Larry Dierker said of Billy's All-Star selection: "I would imagine that he would appreciate it more this year than most."

Somehow, you just know that the gutsy reliever does.

 Billy came back from career-threatening surgery to shine again in 2001. He posted a 2.73 ERA and converted 39 of 41 save opportunities.

>> VLADIMIR GUERRERO

Psst! Want to know a secret? A monster plays in Montreal!

Vladimir Guerrero may be baseball's best–kept secret. Many fans have heard of him, but few have seen him play. That's because the slugging outfielder plays for a team way up in Canada — the Montreal Expos. The Expos rarely appear on national TV in the United States. In a land where hockey is king, the Expos are overshadowed by the famous Montreal Canadiens.

Major leaguers who have seen Vladimir in action can't believe how good he is. St. Louis Cardinal manager Tony La Russa says, "Vladimir's a monster talent. He hits everything. He makes great plays in

the outfield with his tremendous throwing arm. He's an all-around superstar."

Seattle Mariner second baseman Bret Boone says, "In a year or two, Vladimir will be the best player in baseball, hands down."

Even Vladimir's older brother, Wilton, can't believe the things Vladimir can do. "He was always good when we were kids," says Wilton, who once played second base for the Expos. "But not like this."

Vladimir can do it all. He hits for power. He has fleet feet on the base paths. He may have the strongest throwing arm in baseball. He can zip a ball more than 300 feet from deep right field to nail a runner at home plate.

At 6 feet 3 inches and 205 pounds, Vladimir has extremely long arms. When he reaches to stretch before a game, it looks as if he could pluck a cloud right out of the sky. Those long arms allow Vladimir to reach — and hit — almost any pitch. The pitch could be three feet outside the strike zone, but Vladimir will still hit it high and far.

Vladimir's hitting stats are awesome. In 1998, his first full season in the majors, he broke Montreal's single-season team record with 38 home runs. He upped that record to 42 homers in 1999 when he had 131 RBIs and scored more than 100 runs for the second season in a row.

Not bad for someone who was only 23 years old!

THE ONE-SWING WONDER

Vladimir was born on February 9, 1976, in Nizao Bani, a small town in the Dominican Republic. The Guerreros were a big family. Vladimir was one of nine kids. Because his family was poor, Vladimir couldn't afford real baseball equipment. He and Wilton had to play sandlot games with rolled–up socks for balls, a tree limb for a bat, and milk cartons for mitts.

Many kids in the Dominican Republic are poor, but the island country in the Caribbean Sea has produced hundreds of excellent major league players since the 1950s. The weather in the Dominican Republic is usually warm and sunny, so the kids can play ball all year round. Their love of the game helps them overcome obstacles like homemade equipment while they develop their skills simply by playing every day. Scouts from major league teams are always on the lookout for good young players in the Dominican Republic.

Wilton was signed by the Los Angeles Dodgers in 1991, after trying out for one of their scouts. In 1993, Wilton tried to talk the Dodgers into signing Vladimir, too. Vladimir tried out at the team's local baseball academy, but the Dodger scouts thought that he was too skinny, his swing was too wild, and he didn't run fast enough!

VLADIMIR GUERRERO

TEAM	Montreal Expos
POSITION	Outfielder
ACQUIRED	Signed by the Expos as an undrafted, amateur free agent on March 1, 1993
BORN	February 9, 1976, in Nizao Bani, Dominican Republic
HEIGHT	6' 3"
WEIGHT	205 pounds
BATS	Right
THROWS	Right
BIG FEAT	Vladimir hit two homers and had six RBIs against the Philadelphia Phillies on October 2, 1999.
HONORS	N.L. All-Star, 2001, 2000, 1999; N.L. Silver Slugger Award, 2000, 1999; N.L. Gold Glove Eastern League MVP, 1996

The Expos held a tryout later that year. Vladimir was too shy to participate, so he sat on his bicycle and watched from a distance. Finally, the other kids told the Expo scouts that the best player in the neighborhood was that boy over there on the bicycle. The scouts then urged Vladimir to grab a bat. He took one swing, hit the ball, pulled a muscle while running to first base, and couldn't bat anymore. But he still showed enough talent that the Expos gave him $3,500 just to sign a contract!

Vladimir began his pro career that same year in the Dominican Summer League. He shot up through the minor leagues in just three seasons. He was called up to the Expos in September 1996, the season he was named the MVP of the (Double–A) Eastern League.

Vladimir's first full season in the majors, 1997, was expected to be a big one for him. But injuries limited him to just 90 games. He still showed signs of greatness to come by batting .302 with 11 homers and 40 RBIs.

STRANGER IN A STRANGE LAND

While Vladimir was battling injuries on the field, he was struggling with life off it. He had a hard time getting used to daily life in Canada and traveling around the United States on road trips. Vladimir's native language is Spanish. He speaks very little English and no French, which is spoken by many people in Montreal. It was difficult for Vladimir to communicate.

During one road trip, a hotel clerk made a mistake and told Vladimir that he had to check out because his room was needed by an incoming guest. Vladimir couldn't speak English well enough to ask questions or complain, so he packed his bags and put them in his car. Luckily, an Expo team official realized there was a problem and fixed it.

One of Vladimir's best friends during his rookie season with the Expos was pitcher Pedro Martinez, who is now the ace of the Boston Red Sox. Like Vladimir, Pedro is from the Dominican Republic. Pedro wanted to help his countryman. Pedro speaks English very well. He became Vladimir's roommate and taught him some English words and sentences. He also showed Vladimir around the city of Montreal and explained life in the major leagues.

"I care about Vladi like a little brother," Pedro told reporters that season.

Vladimir still needs a translator to give interviews in English. But he now has a much easier time because of Pedro's help. The two players still keep in touch during the season, even though they now play for different teams.

"Pedro took care of me," says Vladimir. "Sometimes, when I was out there playing behind Pedro when he was pitching, I wanted to play really well because I knew how important he was for me."

After Pedro was traded to Boston, Vladimir had a new person to help him: his brother Wilton, who was traded to the Expos from the Los Angeles Dodgers in July 1998. The two brothers spent plenty of time together, especially on road trips. They watched lots of TV — they like comedy movies most of all — and they talked about baseball.

Vladimir also enjoys listening to music on his portable

CD player. On the bus, on the plane, or in the hotel lobby, it doesn't matter — he has his headphones on, the CD player boom–boom–booming music into his ears. Expo pitcher Miguel Batista says, "It's so loud, we tell him, 'You're gonna be deaf in two years.' But he can't hear us. He just smiles."

THE NEW FORCE

It wasn't until 1998 that Vladimir became a force for the Expos. He hit .324 with 38 home runs and 109 RBIs that season. Those were amazing numbers for a 22-year-old player. Only Hall of Famers Mel Ott and Joe DiMaggio have ever had seasons that good while they were that young.

While Vladimir went on tearing the cover off the ball with his bat and terrorizing runners with his arm, the Expos struggled. Montreal had a losing record each season from 1997 to 1999. That kept the spotlight of fame from shining on Vladimir. But he didn't really mind because he doesn't like to call attention to himself.

In 1999, Vladimir went on the longest hitting streak of the season. His streak reached 29 games in a row when he singled against the St. Louis Cardinals on August 24.

When he got that hit, Vladimir was only 15 games away from tying the National League record of 44 that was set by Willie Keeler of Baltimore Orioles in 1897 and tied by Pete Rose of the Cincinnati Reds in 1978. The crowd in Montreal's Olympic Stadium cheered loudly, but Cardinal first baseman Mark McGwire had to urge Vladimir to tip his cap to the fans. Vladimir's hitting streak later ended at 31 games.

Vladimir's 1999 season was the best season by any Expo in the team's history. He set seven new club hitting records, including most RBIs (131) and finished among the N.L. Top 10 hitters in 11 different categories. Vladimir became the first Expo to hit 30 or more home runs and drive in at least 100 RBIs in consecutive seasons. He was unstoppable in August, batting .355 with 12 home runs and 29 RBIs. Vladimir was selected to the N.L. All-Star team.

One of Vladimir's biggest fans was his manager at the time, Felipe Alou. "He's a good late-inning hitter. He gets better as the game progresses, and he gets better as the season progresses," Alou said.

Nobody doubted Coach Alou's assessment of his superstar outfielder, but people were beginning to ask, "Can he possibly get better as his career progresses?"

IN A LEAGUE WITH THE GREATS

Vladimir provided the answer with his bat. Yes, he could — and did — get better. He pounded out a career-high 44 homers, batting at a .345 clip in 2000. His .664 slugging percentage was also the highest of his career. By hitting at least 35 home runs and driving in at least 100 RBIs he joined three Hall of Famers — Joe

Vladimir Guerrero

Experts agree that Vladi has the power and speed to hit 50 homers and steal 50 bases in one season.

Hall of Fame DOUBLE

Frank Robinson was a feared slugger for the Cincinnati Reds, Baltimore Orioles, and three other teams from 1956 to 1976. He had a career .294 batting average and hit 586 homers, fourth-best on the all-time list. He won the "Triple Crown" in 1966 by leading the A.L. in batting (.316), homers (49), and RBIs (122). Vladimir may win a Triple Crown, too. Frank was elected to the Hall of Fame in 1982.

DiMaggio, Ted Williams and Jimmie Foxx — as the only ones to do it before the age of 25. Vladimir was making a name for himself alongside some of the game's greatest players.

Vladimir had started the season on a roll and never looked back. He was named N.L. Player of the Month in April when he hit eight home runs with 27 RBIs, and a sizzling .410 batting average. He finished the season by hitting 13 homers with 26 RBIs in September. In the months between April and September, he was just as deadly. Against the Arizona Diamondbacks on August 8, he tripled and homered twice, setting a personal career high of 11 total bases. He also knocked in four runs in the game.

Vladimir's record-setting season earned him his second consecutive selection to the N.L. All-Star team. Even without the attention that other players received playing for better teams, Vladimir had made believers out of everyone.

"If he played for the Yankees or the Braves, he'd be like (Ken) Griffey (Junior)," said former Expo teammate Rondell White. "He fits into that class anyway. But it would be scary if everybody saw what we've seen him do every day."

CHANGES IN 2001

Vladimir faced new challenges as the 2001 season began. During the off-season, Wilton was traded to the Cincinnati Reds. The Expos' bench coach Luis Pujols, Vladimir's closest friend and mentor, was also gone. He had been fired in July 2000.

Vladimir got off to a slow start batting only .280 in the new season. Some people said it was because Vladimir was missing the positive influences of Wilton and Luis. Then, a few weeks after the season began, long-time Expo manager Alou was fired.

The Expos' new manager, Jeff Torborg, wanted to

shake things up to get the team playing better. He moved Vladimir to the number three spot in the lineup, removing him from his pressure-filled role as cleanup hitter. The switch worked and lit a fire under Vladimir and the Expos.

Once again, he made the N.L. All-Star team. By early August, Vladimir was back in top form, hitting .321 with 28 homers and 79 RBIs. Vladimir also added another dimension to his game by stealing 19 bases — more than he ever had before. His resurgence was having a positive impact on the team, too. The Expos were playing better than they had played in years.

Vladimir closed the book on the 2001 season with 34 homers, 108 RBIs, and a .307 batting average. His career average now stands at a sparkling .319 mark.

SO GOOD, HE'S SCARY

Coach Torborg isn't the only one who raves about Vladimir's ability at the plate. San Francisco Giant pitcher Jason Schmidt once had a scary experience when he faced Vladimir: "He hit a line drive that went by my ear," says Jason. "It scared me. Then I looked back, and the ball was hit so hard that it hit the wall on the fly. That scared me more. And I thought it was a pretty decent pitch!"

Vladimir has the talent to do something truly spectacular, such as becoming the first player to hit 50 homers and steal 50 bases in one season. Many players say that he is so talented he makes the game look easy.

"It's not as easy as people say it is," says Vladimir. "God gave me the talent. But besides the talent, I have the determination to improve."

Improve? Now, that's a scary thought!

Vladi uses his long arms to reach — and crush — almost any pitch.

>>ANDRUW JONES

He may already be baseball's best centerfielder

Pitchers love having Andruw Jones behind them in centerfield. Andruw is like a bloodhound when it comes to tracking down and catching fly balls, no matter where they are hit. Atlanta Brave ace Tom Glavine has marveled at Andruw's dazzling catches and wondered, *How does he do that?*

Naturally, hitters hate the way Andruw keeps robbing them of what appear to be sure hits. "You've got to hit the ball *way* over the fence to get it by him," says New York Met slugger Mike Piazza.

Few players have more talent than Andruw. Along with his eye-popping fielding skills, he has the ability

to swing a strong bat and burn up the basepaths with his speed. Andruw blasted 26 home runs and stole 24 bases in 1999.

BETTER THAN JUNIOR?

Andruw joined the Braves late in the 1996 season, when he was only 19 years old. The word about him then was that he had almost limitless potential, both as a hitter and a fielder. Andruw started well that year and he has improved steadily. By 1999, many people thought he had become the best centerfielder in baseball — even better than the amazing Ken Griffey, Jr.!

"Every time we play against Andruw, he makes a great play against us," says Billy Wagner, the star reliever for the Houston Astros.

Andruw won his first Gold Glove Award for his fielding skills in 1998, when he was 21. He was the youngest player ever to win a Gold Glove. He won another in 1999. "Defense is the most fun part of the game for me," says Andruw. "I take pride in my defense."

Andruw looks so smooth and natural in centerfield that people sometimes wonder if he's trying hard. There have been times when he hasn't hustled, and it has cost him. He was embarrassed when Brave manager Bobby Cox removed him from a 1997 game because he didn't run hard after a fly ball. But Andruw says that "punishment" made him concentrate more during games.

Where does Andruw get his smoothness? If you ask him, he'll say he gets it from his father, Henry, who was a good baseball player, too.

ISLAND CHILD

Andruw was born on April 23, 1977, in the tiny nation of Curaçao [*cur-uh-SOW*]. You'll have a difficult time finding Curaçao on a globe or a map. It is a small island in the Netherlands Antilles, a group of islands in the Caribbean Sea north of Venezuela, South America. Only about 150,000 people live on Curaçao. Just three people from the island have ever become major league baseball players. Andruw is the best of the three, by far.

Andruw grew up in the town of Willemstad, where he learned to speak Dutch, English, and Spanish, along with his native language, Papiamento. He played short–stop, third baseman, and catcher in youth league base–ball. When he ran the bases, Andruw showed flashes of his dad's smooth, natural speed.

"My dad was always a smooth guy," says Andruw. "He acts like he's not running, but he's running. I don't look like I'm running fast, but I still catch the ball."

Major league scouts noticed Andruw's speed and his strong throwing arm. They told him that his professional future was in the outfield, not the infield. So Andruw switched positions.

"It just came naturally," Andruw says about his move to

ANDRUW JONES

TEAM	Atlanta Braves
POSITION	Outfielder
ACQUIRED	Signed by the Braves as an amateur free agent on July 2, 1993
BORN	April 23, 1977, in Willemstad, Curaçao
HEIGHT	6' 1"
WEIGHT	185 pounds
BATS	Right
THROWS	Right
BIG FEAT	In 1996, Andruw became the youngest player to hit a homer in the World Series (age 19, Game 1, against the New York Yankees at Yankee Stadium).
HONORS	N.L. All-Star, 2000; N.L. Gold Glove Award, 2000, 1999, 1998; Named Minor League Player of the Year by Baseball America, 1996, 1995

the outfield. He added, "People say it's easy, but it's not. You have to time fly balls and know where hitters are going to hit the ball. If anyone says it is easy, he's lying."

In 1993, at age 15, Andruw attended a Braves' tryout camp. When Andruw was asked to run a 60-yard dash, his dad decided to run, too! Andruw ran the dash in 6.7 seconds. His dad — who was more than 40 years old —

finished just half a second behind him! The Braves couldn't sign Mr. Jones to a contract, but they made sure to sign Andruw. He started his pro career with the Gulf Coast Braves in 1994. He was 17.

BLAZING SKYROCKET

During his second season of minor league ball, Andruw started making a big impression. He played for the Braves' Class A team in Macon, Georgia, that season. He collected 25 homers, 100 RBIs, and 56 stolen bases. No minor leaguer had put up numbers that good in more than 30 years! *Baseball America* magazine named Andruw the 1995 Minor League Player of the Year.

What did Andruw do for an encore in 1996? He won the award again, as he shot up through the Braves' minor league system like a blazing skyrocket. He played for Class A, Double-A, and Triple-A teams that season. His combined totals were 34 homers, 92 RBIs, and 30 steals with a .339 batting average. The higher Andruw climbed, the better he played . . . and the more people talked about how good he was going to be.

A lot was expected of Andruw when he began his major league career, late in the 1996 season. The Braves' minor league coordinator had told manager Bobby Cox: "When Andruw gets to the big leagues, he'll be an All-Star every year."

The pressure didn't seem to bother Andruw one bit.

He was called up to Atlanta on August 14. He was only 19 years old. He went one-for-five in his first game, drove in a run, and threw out a runner as the Braves beat the Philadelphia Phillies, 8–5. In his second game, Andruw belted a triple and a home run in a 5–4 win over the Pittsburgh Pirates.

MAKING HISTORY

Andruw played so well the rest of the season that the Braves put him on their roster for the World Series. It was a good thing they did. In Game 1, against the New York Yankees, he hit a home run in his first at-bat. The blast made him the youngest player to hit a Series homer, breaking the record that Yankee slugger Mickey Mantle had held since 1952.

Two innings later, Andruw came to bat again — and bashed another homer! He and Gene Tenace of the 1972 Oakland Athletics are the only players in baseball history who have hit homers in their first two World Series at-bats. The Braves won the game, 12–1.

"This is really special for me," Andruw said afterward. "I was nervous when I came up to the big leagues for the first time. But I really wasn't nervous tonight. I just tried to block the fans out and go play."

The Braves lost the Series to the Yankees, four games to two. But Andruw was given a hero's welcome after he flew home to Curaçao. Thousands of fans went to the airport to greet him when he arrived.

Andruw Jones

Andruw easily ranks as one of the top defensive outfielders in the majors.

"It makes me happy because people from Curaçao are happy with me," said Andruw.

Andruw struggled in 1997, his first full season in the major leagues. Opposing pitchers had figured out what pitches would give him the most trouble. Andruw hit only .231 and drove in just 70 runs. But the Braves were patient with their budding star. He worked at correcting his weaknesses and bounced back by having his best season in 1998. That's when he hit .271, with 31 homers, 90 RBIs, and 27 stolen bases. He also won his first Gold Glove.

Andruw helped rescue the Braves in 1999. Their slugging first baseman, Andres Galarraga, was lost for the season due to cancer. Star catcher Javy Lopez was lost in July due to an injury. Andruw helped make up for their absence by hitting a then career–high .275, with 26 homers, and by playing his usual stellar defense. The Braves finished first in their division for the ninth time since 1990, and reached the World Series for the fifth time since 1991.

A BIG DEAL?

After the World Series, Andruw found himself part of the hottest story in sports: The Seattle Mariners were trying to trade Ken Griffey, Jr. The Braves were one of the teams the Mariners had contacted. It was reported that the Mariners were asking for Andruw and pitcher Kevin Millwood in exchange for Ken.

Would the Braves really trade Andruw for the player to whom he is most often compared? Weeks went by.

Christmas came and went. The year 2000 dawned and spring training drew nearer.

Finally, a blockbuster trade was announced in February. Ken was going to the Cincinnati Reds. Andruw was remaining with Atlanta.

Braves' players weren't at all disappointed that Ken didn't come to Atlanta. They knew the kind of player Andruw was — and what he could be. "He hasn't really scratched the surface of what he can do," said Tom Glavine. "He's pretty much doing it just on raw talent."

STRIKING IT RICH

Andruw did a lot more than scratch the surface of his potential in 2000. He struck gold. He put up career highs in batting average (.303), home runs (36), RBIs (104), runs (122), hits (199), and doubles (36). He won his third consecutive N.L. Gold Glove Award and committed just two errors in a major league–high 449 total chances. It was a huge break–out year for the young centerfielder who was selected to the National League All–Star team for the first time.

Andruw's increased productivity came as the result of the long hours that he and Braves' hitting coach Merv Rettunmund put in during spring training. Merv taught Andruw, a notorious pull hitter, how to hit the ball up the middle and to right field. "He can do some amazing things. He's got the ability to hit anywhere he wants in the lineup," Merv said.

Hall of Fame DOUBLE

Willie Mays made playing centerfield look easy, as Andruw does. Willie had the speed to catch any fly ball. He made great throws to nail runners. And, like Andruw, he caught easy flies in his own style — underhand near his waist, with what is called a "basket catch." (Andruw catches balls at his chest.) Both players hit with great power. Willie slammed an amazing 660 homers during his 22-year career (1951 to 1973) with the New York Giants, San Francisco Giants, and New York Mets. He was elected to the Hall of Fame in 1979.

Before the start of the 2000 season, Andruw had said of the Braves, "I think they're waiting for me to have a great, great, great season with my bat. But it's not that easy. I can hit. I just need to make my adjustments."

Little did Andruw know then that he would give the Braves exactly the kind of season they were waiting for.

The Braves made it to the playoffs and faced the St. Louis Cardinals in the N.L. Division Series match-up. The Cardinals upset the Braves, sweeping them in three straight. Andruw batted only .111 with one homer and one RBI. The Braves would have to wait for another trip to the World Series.

Andruw's output during the regular season helped support his request for an increased salary for the year 2001. He was awarded an $8.2 million arbitration decision in February, setting a record for the highest salary decided by an arbitration panel. The award increased his annual salary by $4.5 million. Andruw had earned $3.7 million in 2000.

Teammate Eddie Perez expressed most people's thoughts about the record-setting award: "It's probably a surprise to some people, but not to me. He's [Andruw] the best player we've got, and the best centerfielder I've ever seen," Eddie said.

TIME IS ON HIS SIDE

Even the best players go through periods when they are not making good contact at the plate. Andruw was struggling in 2001 through early August. Although his 23 homers and 72 RBIs were decent numbers, he was batting only .258 and looked uncomfortable in the batter's box. Somehow Andruw had lost the form that made him so successful in 2000. "I just feel maybe a little lazy, not doing the exact things at the plate," he said.

The Braves weren't too concerned with the biggest slump of Andruw's young career. The team won the top spot in the N.L. East Division and Andruw was a major contributor during their pennant drive. In the season, he batted .251 with 34 homers and 104 RBIs. Not too shabby for a guy having an "off year."

Andruw's slump at the plate didn't affect his standing as one of baseball's premier defensive players. Hardly a game went by when he didn't make a spectacular play. As every batter in the N.L. knows, no fly ball is safe when Andruw Jones is after it.

Andruw made an instant splash in 1996 by cracking home runs in his first two World Series at-bats against the Yankess.

>>SHAWN GREEN

Meet a very quiet guy who swings a very loud bat

Shawn Green is quiet and soft–spoken. In the locker room, he loves to read and do crossword puzzles, instead of horsing around and joking loudly with his teammates.

   "Sometimes you don't even notice that Shawn's around," says infielder Homer Bush. Homer was Shawn's teammate on the Toronto Blue Jays in 1999.

   That's not true for major league pitchers who have to face Shawn. They always know that he is around when he swings his Louisville Slugger — *swoosh!* — through the hitting zone. That's because his bat is very loud.

Crack! There goes another line drive past a diving shortstop. *Whack!* There's a sizzling blast off the wall for extra bases. *Smack!* There's a home run over the out-stretched arm of a leaping outfielder.

Shawn is a terrific hitter. The left-handed hitter averaged a crackling .293, with 38 homers, and 112 RBIs per season for Toronto in 1998 and 1999. Shawn's noisy bat attracted the attention of the Los Angeles Dodgers. They traded two players for him in November 1999. The Dodgers liked the fact that Shawn is also an outstanding defensive outfielder and a good base-stealer.

In fact, they liked Shawn's skills so much that they signed him to a six-year, $84 million contract. The contract made Shawn the second-highest paid player in baseball history at the time. Only his Dodger teammate, pitcher Kevin Brown, was earning more money per season. With Kevin on the mound as the ace of the pitching staff and Shawn's bat in the lineup, the Dodgers were piecing together a team that could take them to the World Series.

"I've been an admirer of Shawn Green for a long time," says one-time Dodger manager Davey Johnson. "He's the type of guy who really adds to the whole team with everything he brings."

FIRST LOVE

Shawn was born on November 10, 1972, in Des Plaines, Illinois. His family moved a lot because of his dad's jobs. Mr. Green was a gym teacher, a medical-supplies sales-man, then the owner of the Baseball Academy, in Santa Barbara, California. Santa Barbara is near the town of Tustin, where the Green family settled in 1985. Tustin is about 40 miles from Dodger Stadium in Los Angeles.

It was in Tustin that Shawn fell in love with baseball. He played it every day after school. Because Southern California is usually warm and sunny, Shawn could play year-round, even in the winter.

Shawn's dad taught him a lot about hitting. Mr. Green read books by the famous big-league batting coach Charlie Lau, and passed on the tips to Shawn. They also watched instructional videos and practiced together.

All that attention certainly worked: Shawn hit .717 in Little League one season! By age 12, he was good enough to join a local league for top teenage players. Future major leaguers, such as catcher Mike Lieberthal of the Philadelphia Phillies and outfielder Dmitri Young of the Cincinnati Reds, played in the league. Shawn wel-comed the chance to develop his skills more quickly by playing against older, better players.

"I remember when we gave him his first uniform. He was so skinny!" says John Cole, who was Shawn's

SHAWN GREEN

TEAM	Los Angeles Dodgers
POSITION	Outfielder
ACQUIRED	Traded to the Dodgers by the Toronto Blue Jays for outfielder Raul Mondesi and pitcher Pedro Borbon on November 8, 1999.
BORN	November 10, 1972, in Des Plaines, Illinois
HEIGHT	6' 3"
WEIGHT	200 pounds
BATS	Left
THROWS	Left
BIG FEAT	In 1998, Shawn became the first Blue Jay in Toronto's history to join the "30–30 Club" (hit 30 or more homers and steal 30 or more bases in one season).
HONORS	A.L. All-Star, 1999: N.L. Gold Glove Award, 1999

manager. "But when he played with us, he showed out-standing hand–eye coordination. He could always put the ball in play, no matter who was pitching. You saw a chance in Shawn for an incredibly good future."

HIGH SCHOOL HOTSHOT

That future was right around the corner. Shawn improved so much at Tustin High School that by the time he graduated, in 1991, he was one of the top high school players in America. As a senior, Shawn tied the California Interscholastic Federation record for most hits in one season with 147. He was a first-team selection on *USA Today's* 1991 All-USA High School baseball team. He was also a straight-A student. He received a scholarship offer from Stanford University, in California. Stanford is one of the best colleges in the United States.

The Blue Jays picked Shawn in the first round of the June 1991 draft. The Jays wanted him so much that they gave him $725,000 just to sign a pro contract! At that time, it was the second-highest bonus ever paid to a draft pick. (Pitcher Brien Taylor received $1,550,000 from the New York Yankees in 1989.)

THIN TIMES

The Blue Jays expected a lot from Shawn. But he didn't get off to a strong start in his pro career, partly because of thumb injuries. He hit only .278 with a not-so-grand total of five home runs during his first two minor league seasons (1992 and 1993).

Some of Shawn's problems at the plate were caused by being so thin. He was 6 feet 3 inches tall but weighed only 170 pounds. So Shawn started taking vitamins and working out. He grew bigger and stronger. In 1994, he hit 13 homers for the Syracuse Chiefs, a team in the Triple-A International League. Shawn's batting average soared to .344 — good enough to win the 1994 International League batting title.

Shawn had his first visit to the majors that season. On June 10, he was called up to Toronto. He struggled to hit against left-handed pitchers and batted just .091 in 14 games before he was sent back to the minors for the rest of the season. That brief peek at Shawn was enough to convince Toronto manager Cito Gaston that Shawn would never hit well against lefty pitchers.

Shawn made the Blue Jays' roster in spring training in 1995, but he rarely played when the team faced a lefty. It was a frustrating time for Shawn. Here he was, one of the most talented young players in the major leagues, but he had no chance to really prove it, game in and game out.

Finally, in 1998, that changed. Tim Johnson took over as manager of the Blue Jays. He had a lot of faith in Shawn. Tim believed that with time and experience, Shawn would learn how to handle lefties and become a great all-around player.

Tim wrote Shawn's name on the lineup card every day during the 1998 season, no matter who was pitching for the other team. Shawn hit only .221 with eight

Shawn rebounded in 2001 to give the Dodgers the lift they needed.

Hall of Fame DOUBLE

Shawn reminds baseball fans of Al Kaline because he's such a complete player. Al played rightfield for the Detroit Tigers from 1953 to 1974. Like Shawn, he could hit for average and power, steal bases and play superb defense. Al hit .297, smacked 399 home runs, and made the All-Star team 15 times during his career. He also was a quiet leader in the clubhouse, just like Shawn. Al was elected to the Hall of Fame in 1980.

homers and 31 RBIs against lefties. But he pounded the ball off righties, hitting a healthy .299 with 27 homers against them. In all, Shawn finished the season with a .278 batting average, 35 homers, 100 RBIs, and 35 stolen bases. He had become the Blue Jays' first "30–30" player (a player who hits 30 or more homers and steals 30 or more bases during the same season).

Shawn was still working out. The years he had spent weightlifting helped him bulk up to 200 pounds. That gave him power at the plate.

"I surprised myself by hitting so many homers," says Shawn. "I was always a guy who hit more for average. I was never a home run hitter, from Little League on up. I think I hit three home runs during my senior year of high school. So I never thought of myself as somebody who could do it."

Shawn's bat boomed in 1999. He slugged 42 homers, batted .309, and drove in 123 runs. He also led the American League with 45 doubles and played in his first All-Star Game. Shawn scored 134 runs — the second-best total in the league. During June and July, he had a 28-game hitting streak. That turned out to be the longest streak by any player in the league during the entire season.

ONE OF THE FEW

As Shawn's performance on the field attracted attention from fans and the media, he also became well-known for being one of about 10 Jewish players in the major leagues. Jewish people make up only 6 percent of the population of the United States, and Jewish baseball players are rare. But there have been some great ones in baseball history. Hank Greenberg was a feared slugger for the Detroit Tigers from 1930 to 1946. Sandy Koufax was a great pitcher for the Dodgers from 1955 to 1966. Both players are in the Baseball Hall of Fame.

Jewish fans often walk up to Shawn in cities around

the United States and tell him that he's their hero. Sometimes parents invite him to attend their son's bar mitzvah, which is a special religious ceremony and celebration.

"It's a great feeling to know that so many kids are looking up to me because I'm Jewish," says Shawn. "I understand that being Jewish is something that separates me from most players in baseball and most athletes. That's going to be something I'll be remembered for in my whole career."

HOMETOWN HERO

When he was traded to the Dodgers in November 1999, Shawn was thrilled. He was happy that he would get to play near his home in California. He wanted to give something back to the community, so he decided to donate $250,000 each year to help restore youth baseball fields in the Los Angeles area. He wanted to give more kids the chance to enjoy playing baseball as much as he did when he was a kid.

Shawn contributes a lot of his personal time to youth-oriented causes. He is a spokesperson for Jewish Big Brothers, an organization that matches adult volunteers with Jewish children from single-parent homes. As a role model for kids around the country, Shawn is appreciative of the opportunity to help youngsters. "It's a great cause," Shawn says. "It's important for kids to have mentors to look up to."

DODGER DREAMS

Shawn got his first year with the Dodgers off to a fast start. By the end of May he was hitting .338 with 10 home runs and 39 RBIs. Keeping up that pace would have ensured him of a spot on the National League All–Star team, but Shawn soon found the going a little tough, and his numbers began to drop. By the end of the season, Shawn had posted decent figures, but not what he and the Dodgers were expecting. He finished with a .269 batting average with 24 homers and 99 RBIs.

Even with a slip in his output, Shawn had his share of memorable accomplishments. His 99 RBIs tied the team record for most RBIs by a left–handed hitter in a season. Shawn also hit a hot stretch in which he reached base safely in 53 consecutive games. His ability to hit in the clutch was in evidence as he batted .467 (7 for 15) with three doubles, two home runs, and 21 RBIs with the bases loaded.

REBIRTH OF THE DODGER BLUE

"I didn't feel in control of my at–bats," Shawn said about his 2000 performance. "A lot of times I felt defensive at the plate. The two previous years, I felt in charge. That's all I want. That's what I'm looking for this year — 2001 — to feel in charge. The numbers will come."

Shawn wasn't kidding. The numbers did come in 2001.

At the beginning of August, he had already hit 31 home runs — seven more than all of 2000 — and drove in 87 runs. His batting was .288 and his slugging percentage was one of the highest of his career.

The Dodgers reaped the benefits of Shawn's resurgence. They were leading the N.L. West Division and battling for a playoff spot. After finishing 11 games out of first place in 2000, the Dodgers were back in the thick of a pennant race.

Ultimately, Los Angeles started to fade in the final weeks of the season, but Shawn showed no signs of slowing down. He smacked 49 homers and knocked in 125 runs to go along with a .297 average.

It was no coincidence that the turnabout in Dodgers' fortunes came at the same time of Shawn's increased productivity. In one rapid-fire burst of power, Shawn hit home runs in five consecutive games to equal a franchise record. The last player to do this was Hall of Famer Roy Campanella of the old Brooklyn Dodgers in 1950.

Shawn has been compared to Hall of Famer Ted Williams, by his Dodger hitting coach, Manny Mota. "Ted Williams had what Shawn has. He was a natural. Shawn's a natural, too," Manny says.

That's mighty high praise.

Shawn has one of the most graceful swings in baseball.
His stats are just as pretty.

>>ALEX RODRIGUEZ

He's done a lot of awesome things in a short time

Shortstop Alex Rodriguez of the Seattle Mariners was living a charmed life. At 17, he was the Number 1 pick in the baseball draft. At 18, he was in the major leagues. By the tender age of 20, he was on his way to · becoming a superstar. Not only was he an All–Star by age 21, but — like Derek Jeter of the New York Yankees — "A–Rod" had become a fan heartthrob. Girls loved his movie–star good looks, and everybody who followed baseball admired his talent and success.

Then it happened.

Alex was doing agility exercises in spring training, just days before the beginning of the 1999 season. He

jumped over a box, fell, and tore a ligament in his left knee. He needed surgery and missed the next five weeks of the season. It was the first major mishap of Alex's career and the first time he had ever had surgery. He was stunned. "I never thought it would happen to me," said Alex.

It had happened, so the question became: Would Alex be able to play at his usual high level when he returned to the diamond? Some people, including Alex, were not sure.

But two of his teammates — Jay Buhner and Edgar Martinez — reassured Alex that he would be okay. They had gone through surgery themselves and come back. Fans also wrote to Alex, telling him to keep his chin up.

"I got so many letters from doctors and lawyers and people who said they had had the same surgery and that I would be back in no time," says Alex. "That was very encouraging."

AS GOOD AS NEW

Alex worked out hard to get back into shape. When he returned to the Mariners in the middle of May, he began to play like his old super self. He blasted a mon-strous 437-foot homer against the San Diego Padres in June. By the All-Star Game in July, he had hit two homers in one game four times. A-Rod was A-okay!

Alex had faced his toughest challenge and come out on top. "It's very hard to come back after you're injured," he says. "But I had to keep believing in myself. I kept telling myself I'd be as good as new."

He had that right. Alex finished the 1999 season with 42 home runs, which tied for fifth in the American League — despite having missed those five weeks. He also had 111 RBIs and a .285 batting average. He stole 21 bases and would have stolen more if he hadn't been nervous about hurting his knee again.

It turned out to be another amazing season from an amazing player. Alex is so good that some fans think he's the best player in baseball. And Alex is young: he turned 26 years old in 2001.

"I can't wait 'till I hit my prime," says Alex.

AWESOME POWER

Alex can do just about everything on a baseball field, but the thing that sets him apart from other shortstops is his awesome power at the plate. Traditionally, teams expect shortstops to just be good fielders and to maybe run the bases well. But Alex can go deep, like the best sluggers in the game.

"I've watched A-Rod hit homers to leftfield, centerfield, and rightfield," says Sean Casey, the first baseman for the Cincinnati Reds. "He makes it look so easy."

Alex mashed 148 taters during his first four-plus seasons in the majors. That's far more home runs than any shortstop under age 25 had ever hit in the history of baseball. In fact, when Alex hit 42 homers in 1998, it was

ALEX RODRIGUEZ

TEAM	Texas Rangers
POSITION	Shortstop
ACQUIRED	Chosen by the Seattle Mariners in the first round (first player chosen overall) of the major league draft on June 3, 1993; signed by the Texas Rangers, December 11, 2000
BORN	July 27, 1975, in New York, New York
HEIGHT	6' 3"
WEIGHT	195 pounds
BATS	Right
THROWS	Right
BIG FEAT	In 2001, Alex set the Major League record for the most home runs in one season by a shortstop. He hit 52 home runs that season.
HONORS	A.L. All-Star, 2001, 2000, 1998, 1997, 1996; A.L. Silver Slugger Award, 1999, 1998, 1996

the most ever in one season by an American League shortstop. He tied his own home run record in 1999.

Shortstop Omar Vizquel of the Cleveland Indians thinks Alex could hit homers like Barry Bonds if that's what Alex wanted to do. "I think Alex has a chance to break the [single-season] home-run record," says Omar.

AWESOME ALL-AROUND

Alex can do more than hit homers. He stole 46 bases along with his 42 home runs in 1998 to become just the third member of the "40–40" club (players who hit 40 or more homers and steal 40 or more bases in one season). Barry Bonds of the San Francisco Giants and Jose Canseco of the Chicago White Sox are the other two.

Alex also hits for a high average and plays sharp defense. Good as he is, he is always striving to improve.

"I have such a long way to go," says Alex. "Unless you hit one thousand and make no errors, you can always improve in this game."

Other players think Alex is awfully good already.

"He's the best ballplayer in the game," first baseman David Segui of the Baltimore Orioles told the *Seattle Post-Intelligencer* newspaper. "Definitely, Barry Bonds and Ken Griffey, Jr., are up there with him, but the way Alex plays the game sets him apart from everyone else. He plays the game with great intensity, the way it's sup- posed to be played — to win. The way he goes about it day in and day out, with a desire to get better . . . it's very impressive."

Even Derek Jeter, the New York Yankees' star shortstop, is an A–Rod fan. Says Derek: "He's one of the fastest players in the league. I told him he should go for 50–50."

Alexander Emmanuel Rodriguez was born on July 27, 1975, in New York City. He has an older brother, Joe, and a sister, Susy. His parents are from the Dominican Republic, a small island nation in the Caribbean Sea. The family moved back to the Dominican Republic when Alex was 4 years old. Victor Rodriguez, Alex's father, was a catcher in a Dominican professional league. He introduced Alex to baseball.

After four years in the Dominican Republic, the family moved to Kendall, Florida, near Miami. But Alex's father abandoned the family when Alex was 10. Alex kept hoping his dad would return, but he never did. "It was hard," says Alex. "I did my best to help out around the house and bring home good grades to make my mom proud."

MAMA'S PRIDE

Alex made his mom, Lourdes Rodriguez, proud in many ways. He became an honor student at Westminster Christian School and the best high school baseball player in the United States. Westminster won the 1992 national high school championship when Alex was a junior. He hit a hefty .450 that season.

The following year, Alex batted a monstrous .505 and swiped 35 bases in 35 attempts. But everything did not go right: Alex made a crucial throwing error that helped cost his team a chance to win the national championship again. "That was real hard to come back from," he says. "But I had to put it behind me."

The Seattle Mariners made it easier for Alex to move on. They had the first pick in baseball's 1993 amateur draft and could have picked any high school or college player in the country. The Mariners chose Alex.

After less than one season in the minor leagues, Alex was called up to Seattle in July 1994. At age 18, he was the youngest starting shortstop in the majors since 1974, when Hall of Famer Robin Yount started for the Milwaukee Brewers. But when Alex hit only .204 in 17 games, the Mariners decided that he wasn't quite ready for prime time. They shifted him back and forth between Seattle and the minor leagues all season in 1995.

ONE-MAN WRECKING CREW

It wasn't until spring training of 1996 that Alex, who was still only 20 years old, became the Mariners' starting shortstop for good. He was a one-man wrecking crew that season. He led the majors with a .358 batting average, blasted 36 home runs, and finished a close second to then-Texas Ranger outfielder Juan Gonzalez in the voting for the American League MVP award.

"I think it was a surprise for everyone," Alex says about his breakout season. "It certainly was a pleasant surprise for me."

Alex's numbers slipped to 23 homers with 84 RBIs and a .300 batting average in 1997. He was selected to the A.L. All-Star team for the second year in a row and there was little doubt around the league that he would be one of the premier players for years to come. His selection as the starting shortstop in the All-Star Game broke Cal Ripken, Jr.'s streak of 13 straight starts at the position. Alex was at the head of a youth movement sweeping through major league baseball.

Alex says that watching Ken Griffey, Jr., play every day helped him succeed quickly in the majors. The two teammates became friends who even played video games together. "Ken teaches you that you can have fun, respect the game, and also play it hard," says Alex. "When you have that combination, you're going to put yourself in a position to be successful."

Says Ken: "Alex works hard. He's a smart kid. Everyone knows he's going to be a special player."

A PAIN IN THE KNEE

Alex showed everyone just how special he was in 2000. He opened the season on a tear, batting .405 in his first 12 games. By mid-season, he was batting .345 with 24 homers and 78 RBIs. Alex was selected for the 2000 All-Star team, but a pair of injuries kept him from playing in the game.

On July 7, he was knocked unconscious in a collision with Los Angeles Dodger shortstop Alex Cora in an interleague game. He collided with Cora in a play at second base while trying to break up a double play.

Ranger fans have lots to cheer about with perennial All-Star Alex Rodriguez in the lineup.

Hall of Fame DOUBLE

Like Alex, Honus Wagner could do it all. Honus played shortstop for the Pittsburgh Pirates from 1900 to 1917. He had a career batting average of .327 and won eight batting titles. He also led the National League in RBIs five times and stole more than 40 bases in a season eight years in a row. Honus hit few home runs because he played in what was called the "dead-ball" era. He was elected to the Hall of Fame in 1936.

Alex sustained a concussion and a strained right knee that not only prevented him from playing in the All–Star Game, but forced him to miss 13 games.

Once back in the lineup, Alex didn't waste any time picking up where he left off. In his first 15 games back in action, he batted at a .377 clip. On the year, Alex posted some of the best numbers of his career, batting .316 with 41 homers and 132 RBIs, a career high. He also drew 100 walks, by far the best in his career.

Alex and the Mariners won the American League wild card spot and swept the Chicago White Sox in their division championship series. The Mariners then took on the defending world champion New York Yankees. The Yanks beat Seattle in the ALCS, four games to two.

Alex batted .409 with two homers and five RBIs in the loss to the Yankees, giving him an overall batting average of .371 in both series. The Mariners had provided the Yankees with their toughest playoff challenge even though New York went on to win the World Series. With Alex as the backbone of the club, Seattle had established itself as a powerhouse team of the future.

IN GOOD COMPANY

While establishing himself as one of the elite players in the majors, Alex became friends with such elite players as Derek Jeter and Baltimore Oriole great Cal Ripken, Jr. Alex looked up to Cal while growing up and was invited to play one-on-one basketball against Cal a few years ago in the gym at Cal's house. Each player won one game. Says Cal: "He dunked a few times, but not on me. I fouled him before I let him dunk on me!"

Alex and Derek are pals. When Alex would visit New York to play the Yankees, he would often stay at Derek's apartment. Says Derek: "We enjoy competing. When he hits a homer, he sits on the bench and flexes his arms at me."

HOME, HOME ON THE RANGE

At the end of the 2000 season, Alex's contract with the Mariners was up. He became a free agent who could negotiate a new deal with any team he chose. Clubs were lining up to sign him, including the Mariners. The New York Mets were interested. So were the Colorado Rockies and the Texas Rangers. But whoever signed Alex would have to pay handsomely for his all-star services.

As the weeks during the off-season passed, baseball fans closely followed the story of where Alex would play in 2001. Finally, the Texas Rangers won the bidding war and signed Alex to a $252 million, 10-year deal. Alex was now the highest paid baseball player in history. Mariners' fans were plenty disappointed — and many were angry — that Alex had left the team to earn more money somewhere else.

Expectations for Alex were astronomical. The Rangers had never made it past the first round of the playoffs, and all eyes were on Alex to get them over the hump. Rangers' owner Tom Hicks said, "Alex is the player we believe will allow this franchise to fulfill its dream of continuing on its path to becoming a World Series champion."

Playing in Texas was going to be the biggest challenge of Alex's career.

A SOUR OPENING

With the entire baseball world closely looking on, the Rangers opened the 2001 season against the Toronto Blue Jays. The day had come for Alex to make his heralded debut in a Texas uniform. In his first fielding chance of the season, he made a throwing error. On the very next play, he stumbled on a seam in the artificial turf. As if that wasn't bad enough, Alex later tripped on his loose shoelace and fell again. It wasn't all bad, though. He had a pair of singles, including the season's first major league hit.

"You have to start somewhere. There was a little bit of everything: an error, a slip, hits. But it's only one game. There's one-hundred-sixty-one more. You just move on," Alex said.

Move on is exactly what he did. Two weeks later, Alex brought his .341 batting average to Seattle's SafeCo Field. He was going to play in front of Mariners' fans for the first time in a Rangers' uniform. Every time he stepped to the plate, many Seattle fans booed loudly or chanted "Pay-Rod!" They were still angry that he left for greener pastures in Texas. Some fans even threw fake money from the upper decks.

Alex didn't let the razzing upset him. "I think it's all in fun. That's why they're some of the greatest fans. They were in post-season form. If I was wearing a Mariners' uniform tonight, they would have been cheering for me," he said.

MIRED IN LAST PLACE

Some Mariners' fans might have been holding a grudge toward Alex, but Rangers' fans were delighted he was in Texas. Alex was selected to the All-Star team for the fifth time and his numbers by early August ranked with some of the best of his career. Alex was batting .321 with 33 homers and 99 RBIs.

All would have been well in Texas had it not been for the Rangers' terrible performance as a team. They were last in the A.L. West, far behind the division-leading Mariners. Alex's financial fortunes might have taken a positive swing when he signed with the Rangers, but he was now playing for a team mired in the cellar of their division.

However, even in the worst of times, Alex has maintained his professional approach to the game. With his talent and maturity, he is sure to be on top again.

In 2001, Alex continued to make history with his booming bat. He crushed 52 homers, knocked in 135 runs, and batted .318.

CAREER STATS

 Derek Jeter

YEAR	TEAM	GAMES	AB	R	H	2B	3B	HR	RBI	AVG
1995	NY Yankees	15	48	5	12	4	1	0	7	.250
1996	NY Yankees	157	582	104	183	25	6	10	78	.314
1997	NY Yankees	159	654	116	190	31	7	10	70	.291
1998	NY Yankees	149	626	127	203	25	8	19	84	.324
1999	NY Yankees	158	627	134	219	37	9	24	102	.349
2000	NY Yankees	148	593	119	201	31	4	15	73	.339
2001	NY Yankees	150	614	110	191	35	3	21	74	.311

 Kevin Millwood

YEAR	TEAM	GAMES	W	L	IP	SAVES	BB	SO	ERA
1997	Atlanta	12	5	3	51.1	0	21	42	4.03
1998	Atlanta	31	17	8	174.1	0	56	163	4.08
1999	Atlanta	33	18	7	228.0	0	59	205	2.68
2000	Atlanta	36	10	13	212.2	0	62	168	4.66
2001	Atlanta	21	7	7	121.0	0	40	84	4.31

Sean Casey

YEAR	TEAM	GAMES	AB	R	H	2B	3B	HR	RBI	AVG
1997	Cleveland	6	10	1	2	0	0	0	1	.200
1998	Cincinnati	96	302	44	82	21	1	7	52	.272
1999	Cincinnati	151	594	103	197	42	3	25	99	.332
2000	Cincinnati	133	480	69	151	33	2	20	85	.315
2001	Cincinnati	145	533	69	165	40	0	13	89	.310

Nomar Garciaparra

YEAR	TEAM	GAMES	AB	R	H	2B	3B	HR	RBI	AVG
1996	Boston	24	87	11	21	2	3	4	16	.241
1997	Boston	153	684	122	209	44	11	30	98	.306
1998	Boston	143	604	111	195	37	8	35	122	.323
1999	Boston	135	532	103	190	42	4	27	104	.357
2000	Boston	140	529	104	197	51	3	21	96	.372
2001	Boston	21	83	13	24	3	0	4	8	.289

Jason Kendall

YEAR	TEAM	GAMES	AB	R	H	2B	3B	HR	RBI	AVG
1996	Pittsburgh	130	414	54	124	23	5	3	42	.300
1997	Pittsburgh	144	486	71	143	36	4	8	49	.294
1998	Pittsburgh	149	535	95	175	36	3	12	75	.327
1999	Pittsburgh	78	280	61	93	20	3	8	41	.332
2000	Pittsburgh	152	579	112	185	33	6	14	58	.320
2001	Pittsburgh	157	606	84	161	22	2	10	53	.266

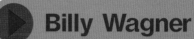 # Billy Wagner

YEAR	TEAM	GAMES	W	L	IP	SAVES	BB	SO	ERA
1995	Houston	1	0	0	0.1	0	0	0	0.00
1996	Houston	37	2	2	51.2	9	30	67	2.44
1997	Houston	62	7	8	66.1	23	30	106	2.85
1998	Houston	58	4	3	60.0	30	25	97	2.70
1999	Houston	66	4	1	74.2	39	23	124	1.57
2000	Houston	28	2	4	27.2	6	18	28	6.18
2001	Houston	64	2	5	62.2	39	20	79	2.73

 # Vladimir Guerrero

YEAR	TEAM	GAMES	AB	R	H	2B	3B	HR	RBI	AVG
1996	Montreal	9	27	2	5	0	0	1	1	.185
1997	Montreal	90	325	44	98	22	2	11	40	.302
1998	Montreal	159	623	108	202	37	7	38	109	.324
1999	Montreal	160	610	102	193	37	5	42	131	.316
2000	Montreal	154	571	101	197	28	11	44	123	.345
2001	Montreal	159	599	107	184	45	4	34	108	.307

 # Andruw Jones

YEAR	TEAM	GAMES	AB	R	H	2B	3B	HR	RBI	AVG
1996	Atlanta	31	106	11	23	7	1	5	13	.217
1997	Atlanta	153	399	60	92	18	1	18	70	.231
1998	Atlanta	159	582	89	158	33	8	31	90	.271
1999	Atlanta	162	592	97	163	35	5	26	84	.275
2000	Atlanta	161	656	122	199	36	6	36	104	.303
2001	Atlanta	161	625	104	157	25	2	34	104	.251

Shawn Green

YEAR	TEAM	GAMES	AB	R	H	2B	3B	HR	RBI	AVG
1993	Toronto	3	6	0	0	0	0	0	0	.000
1994	Toronto	14	33	1	3	1	0	0	1	.091
1995	Toronto	121	379	52	109	31	4	15	54	.288
1996	Toronto	132	422	52	118	32	3	11	45	.280
1997	Toronto	135	429	57	123	22	4	16	53	.287
1998	Toronto	158	630	106	175	33	4	35	100	.278
1999	Toronto	153	614	134	190	45	0	42	123	.309
2000	Los Angeles	162	610	98	164	44	4	24	99	.269
2001	Los Angeles	161	619	121	184	31	4	49	125	.297

Alex Rodriguez

YEAR	TEAM	GAMES	AB	R	H	2B	3B	HR	RBI	AVG
1994	Seattle	17	54	4	11	0	0	0	2	.204
1995	Seattle	48	142	15	33	6	2	5	19	.232
1996	Seattle	146	601	141	215	54	1	36	123	.358
1997	Seattle	141	587	100	176	40	3	23	84	.300
1998	Seattle	161	686	123	213	35	5	42	124	.310
1999	Seattle	129	502	110	143	25	0	42	111	.285
2000	Seattle	148	554	134	175	34	2	41	132	.316
2001	Texas	162	632	133	201	34	1	52	135	.318

>>GLOSSARY

arbitration the process of allowing an impartial person or group to settle a dispute

draft the process of selecting someone from a group of people

Gold Glove Award an honor given to the best fielder at each position in both the National and American Leagues

Hall of Fame an institute located in Cooperstown, New York, to which the greatest baseball players of all time are chosen as members

negotiate to talk about something in the hopes of coming to an agreement

Silver Slugger Award the honor given to the best hitter at each position in both the National and American Leagues

>> RESOURCES

BOOKS

Buckley, Jr., James. *Super Shortstops.* New York: DK Publishing, 2001.

Egan, Terry. *Heroes of the Game.* Minneapolis, MN: Econo–Clad Books, 1997.

Kramer, A. *Baseball's Greatest Hitters.* New York: Random House Books for Young Readers, 2000.

Stewart, Mark. *Alex Rodriguez: Gunning for Greatness.* Brookfield, CT: Millbrook Press, 1999.

Sullivan, George. *Sluggers: Twenty-Seven of Baseball's Greatest.* Old Tappan, NJ: Simon & Schuster Children's, 1999.

MAGAZINES

Baseball Digest
990 Grove Avenue
Evanston, IL 60201
(847) 864–1840
http://www.centurysports.net/baseball

ESPN Magazine
19 East 34th Street
New York, NY 10016
(212) 515–1000
http://espn.go.com

>>RESOURCES

USA TODAY Baseball Weekly
Subscription Processing Center
P.O. Box 4500
Silver Spring, MD 20997–1401
http://www.usatoday.com/sports/mlb.htm

Sports Illustrated For Kids
135 West 50th Street
New York, NY 10020
(800) 992–0196
http://www.sikids.com

WEB SITES

The Official Site of Major League Baseball
http://www.mlb.com
Learn about your favorite teams and players. This Web site has all of the up–to–date information about stand-ings, scores, and statistics.

Baseball–Reference.com
http://www.baseball-reference.com
This site has statistics for teams and individual players, articles, and lots of the historical background of baseball.

RESOURCES

The Sporting News: Baseball
http://www.sportingnews.com/baseball/
Follow your favorite teams and players throughout the season on this informative Web site.

Sports Illustrated: Baseball
http://sportsillustrated.cnn.com/baseball/
This site has all of the current standings, statistics, and scores. It also has informative articles and discussions throughout the season.

Yahoo! Sports: Major League Baseball
http://sports.yahoo.com/mlb/
Find out the latest MLB news on this informative site.

SPORTS ILLUSTRATED FOR KIDS
http://www.sikids.com
Check out the latest sports news, cool games, and much more.

>>RESOURCES

ORGANIZATIONS

National Baseball Hall of Fame and Museum
25 Main Street
P.O. Box 590
Cooperstown, NY 13326
Phone: (888) 425–5633
Fax: (607) 547–2044
http://www.baseballhalloffame.org

>>INDEX